National Curriculum Standards for

I Culture

Social studies programs should include experiences that provide for the study of culture and cultural diversity.

II Time, Continuity, & Change

Social studies programs should include experiences that provide for the study of the ways human beings view themselves in and over time while recognizing examples of change and cause and effect relationships.

III People, Places, & Environments

Social studies programs should include experiences that provide for the study of people, places, and environments.

IV Individual Development & Identity

Social studies programs should include experiences that provide for the study of individual development and identity while recognizing personal changes over time and personal connections to places.

V Individuals, Groups, & Institutions

Social studies programs should include experiences that provide for the study of interactions among individuals, groups, and institutions while giving examples of and explaining, group and institutional influences on people, events, and elements of culture.

VI Power, Authority, & Governance

Social studies programs should include experiences that provide for the study of how people create and change structures of power, authority, and governance while examining the rights and responsibilities of the individual in relation to his or her social group.

VII Production, Distribution, & Consumption

Social studies programs should include experiences that provide for the study of how people organize for the production, distribution, and consumption of goods and services.

VIII Science, Technology, & Society

Social studies programs should include experiences that provide for the study of relationships among science, technology, and society.

IX Global Connections

Social studies programs should include experiences that provide for the study of global connections and independence while giving examples of conflict, cooperation, and interdependence among individuals, groups, and nations.

X Civic Ideals & Practices

Social studies programs should include experiences that provide for the study of the ideals, principles, and practices of citizenship in a democratic republic.

National Geography Standards

The *Geographically Informed Person* knows and understands . . .

THE WORLD IN SPATIAL TERMS

STANDARD 1: How to use maps and other geographic representations, tools, and technologies to acquire, process, and report information.

STANDARD 2: How to use mental maps to organize information about people, places, and environments.

STANDARD 3: How to analyze the spatial organization of people, places, and environments on Earth's surface.

PLACES AND REGIONS

STANDARD 4: The physical and human characteristics of places.

STANDARD 5: That people create regions to interpret Earth's complexity.

STANDARD 6: How culture and experience influence people's perception of places and regions.

PHYSICAL SYSTEMS

STANDARD 7: The physical processes that shape the patterns of Earth's surface.

STANDARD 8: The characteristics and spatial distribution of ecosystems on Earth's surface.

HUMAN SYSTEMS

STANDARD 9: The characteristics, distribution, and migration of human populations on Earth's surface.

STANDARD 10: The characteristics, distributions, and complexity of Earth's cultural mosaics.

STANDARD 11: The patterns and networks of economic interdependence on Earth's surface.

STANDARD 12: The process, patterns, and functions of human settlement.

STANDARD 13: How forces of cooperation and conflict among people influence the division and control of Earth's surface.

ENVIRONMENT AND SOCIETY

STANDARD 14: How human actions modify the physical environment.

STANDARD 15: How physical systems affect human systems.

STANDARD 16: The changes that occur in the meaning, use, distribution, and importance of resources.

THE USES OF GEOGRAPHY

STANDARD 17: How to apply geography to interpret the past.

STANDARD 18: To apply geography to interpret the present and plan for the future.

Macmillan/McGraw-Hill TIMELINKS

Our Country and Its Regions

PROGRAM AUTHORS

James A. Banks
Kevin P. Colleary
Linda Greenow
Walter C. Parker
Emily M. Schell
Dinah Zike

CONTRIBUTORS

Raymond C. Jones
Irma M. Olmedo

 Macmillan/McGraw-Hill

Volume 2

PROGRAM AUTHORS

James A. Banks, Ph.D.
Kerry and Linda Killinger
  Professor of Diversity Studies
  and Director, Center for
  Multicultural Education
University of Washington
Seattle, Washington

Kevin P. Colleary, Ed.D.
Curriculum and Teaching
  Department
Graduate School of Education
Fordham University
New York, New York

Linda Greenow, Ph.D.
Associate Professor and Chair
Department of Geography
State University of New York at
  New Paltz
New Paltz, New York

Walter C. Parker, Ph.D.
Professor of Social Studies
  Education, Adjunct Professor
  of Political Science
University of Washington
Seattle, Washington

Emily M. Schell, Ed.D.
Visiting Professor, Teacher
  Education
San Diego State University
San Diego, California

Dinah Zike
Educational Consultant
Dinah-Mite Activities, Inc.
San Antonio, Texas

CONTRIBUTORS

Raymond C. Jones, Ph.D.
Director of Secondary Social
  Studies Education
Wake Forest University
Winston-Salem, North Carolina

Irma M. Olmedo
Associate professor
University of Illinois-Chicago
College of Education
Chicago, Illinois

HISTORIANS/SCHOLARS

Ned Blackhawk
Associate Professor of History
  and American Indian Studies
University of Wisconsin
Madison, Wisconsin

Sheilah F. Clarke-Ekong, Ph.D.
Professor of Anthropology
University of Missouri-St. Louis
St. Louis, Missouri

Larry Dale, Ph.D.
Director, Center for Economic
  Education
Arkansas State University
Jonesboro, Arkansas

Brooks Green, Ph.D.
Associate Professor of
  Geography
University of Central Arkansas
Conway, Arkansas

Thomas C. Holt, Ph.D.
Professor of History
University of Chicago
Chicago, Illinois

Students with print disabilities may be eligible to obtain an accessible, audio version of the pupil edition of this textbook. Please call Recording for the Blind & Dyslexic at 1-800-221-4792 for complete information.

The **McGraw-Hill** Companies

Macmillan McGraw-Hill

Send all inquires to:
Macmillan/McGraw-Hill
8787 Orion Place
Columbus, OH 43240-4027

MHID 0-02-152404-1
ISBN 978-0-02-152404-4
Printed in the United States of America.
4 5 6 7 8 9 10   DOW/LEH   13 12 11 10 09

Our Country and Its Regions
CONTENTS, Volume 2

Reference Section

Skills and Features

Maps

Unit 3

EXPLORE The Big Idea

Essential Question
What causes a region to change?

FOLDABLES Study Organizer

Main Idea and Details
Use a layered book foldable to take notes as you read Unit 3. The title of the foldable should be **The Northeast**. Label the three tabs **Geography**, **Economy**, and **People**.

People
Economy
Geography
The Northeast

LOG ON
For more about Unit 3 go to www.macmillanmh.com

The Northeast

PEOPLE, PLACES, AND EVENTS

Native American Dance and Music Festival

The Iroquois People

The Eastern Woodlands were once home to many groups of Native Americans. One large group, **the Iroquois people**, partnered with five Native American groups.

Today visit the Ganondagan State Historic Site and attend the **Native American Dance and Music Festival**.

Immigrants

Ellis Island

The United States began to grow rapidly in the late 1800s. **Immigrants** arrived looking for a better life. After 1892, most immigrants entered the United States through the immigration center on **Ellis Island** in New York harbor.

Today you can visit Ellis Island and learn about immigration.

LOG ON

For more about People, Places, and Events, visit:
www.macmillanmh.com.

Harlem in New York City

African Americans

In the early 1900s, thousands of **African Americans** moved north in the Great Migration to find work. Many settled in Newark, New Jersey, and **Harlem in New York City**.

Today you can learn more about African American communities at the Anacostia Community Museum in Washington, D.C.

Boothbay Harbor, Maine

Annual Fisherman's Festival

Along much of the Northeast coast, small villages and towns grew out of the fishing industry. One of these is **Boothbay Harbor, Maine**.

Today you can celebrate Boothbay Harbor's heritage as a fishing village during the **Annual Fisherman's Festival**.

Northeast Region

The Northeast is home to exciting places like our nation's capital.

1 Snowboarding is a popular winter activity in the mountains of the Northeast.

Lake Erie

6 Pennsylvania is home to one of the world's largest chocolate factories—Hershey's Chocolate World.

5 Cape Cod, Massachusetts, is a popular destination.

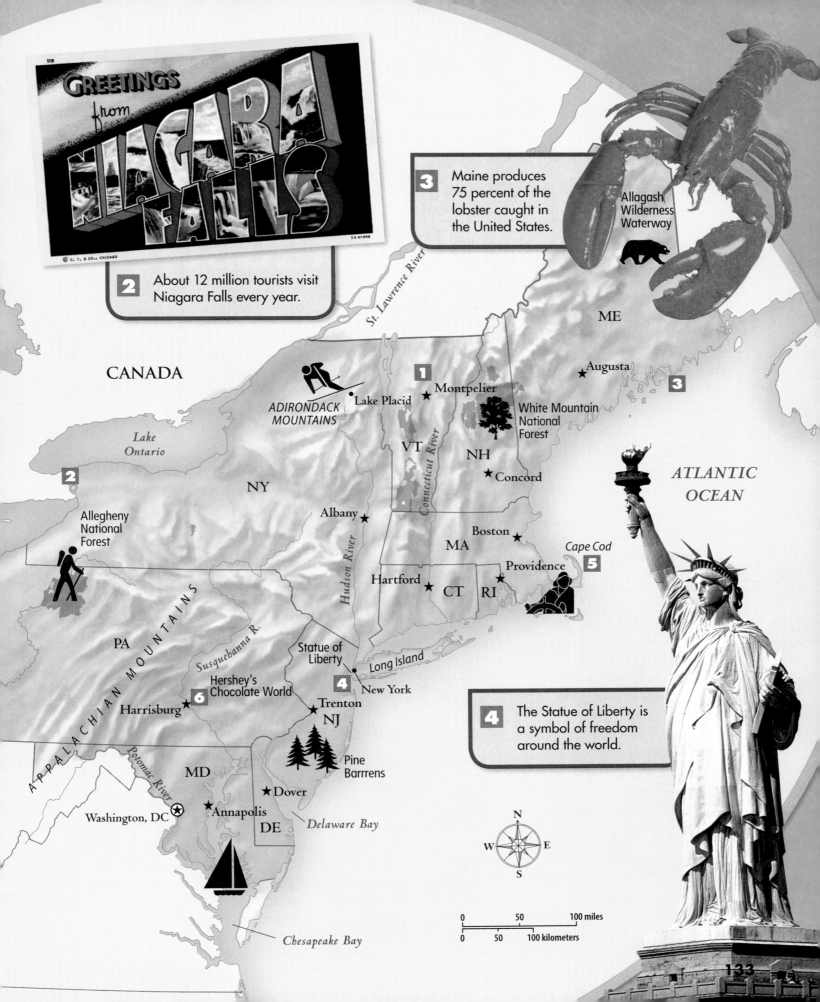

Greetings from NIAGARA FALLS

119

© C. T. & CO. CHICAGO

5A-H1968

2 About 12 million tourists visit Niagara Falls every year.

3 Maine produces 75 percent of the lobster caught in the United States.

Allagash Wilderness Waterway

ME

CANADA

1 Montpelier ★

Augusta ★

3

ADIRONDACK MOUNTAINS
Lake Placid ●

White Mountain National Forest

Lake Ontario

2

VT

NH

Concord ★

NY

Allegheny National Forest

ATLANTIC OCEAN

Albany ★

Boston ●

Cape Cod

Connecticut River

MA

Providence

5

Hudson River

Hartford ★

CT

RI

St. Lawrence River

PA

APPALACHIAN MOUNTAINS

Susquehanna R.

Statue of Liberty

Long Island

New York

4

Hershey's Chocolate World

Harrisburg ★

6

Trenton ★

NJ

Pine Barrrens

Potomac River

MD

★ Dover

Washington, DC ✪

★ Annapolis

DE

Delaware Bay

4 The Statue of Liberty is a symbol of freedom around the world.

N
W   E
S

0   50   100 miles
0   50   100 kilometers

Chesapeake Bay

133

The Geography of the Northeast

VOCABULARY

glacier p. 135

bay p. 136

fuel p. 136

fall line p. 138

tourist p. 140

READING SKILL

Main Idea and Details
Copy the chart below. Fill it in with details about how the Northeast was formed.

Main Idea	Details

STANDARDS FOCUS

SOCIAL STUDIES — People, Places, and Environments

GEOGRAPHY — The Uses of Geography

Visual Preview

How has the geography of the Northeast affected the region?

A Animals and plants live in the Northeast, which was shaped by glaciers.

B Cities grew around bays because they provided protection for ships.

C The Northeast has many natural resources that include forests and water.

D The Northeast has four seasons.

A THE NORTHEAST LONG AGO

The 11 states that make up the Northeast share a rich geography, sprinkled with mountains, hills, lakes, rivers, and forests. Most of them were formed long ago.

The world's oldest chain of mountains, the Appalachians, stretches from Maine in the North to Alabama in the South. The mountains were formed more than 250 million years ago. Year after year of wind, water, and ice eroded their sharp and pointed peaks into rolling hills. The Appalachians saw a good deal of bad weather many years ago. Today the Northeast still experiences harsh weather.

The Ice Was Here

Once, much of northern North America was covered with large, moving sheets of ice called **glaciers**. In some places, these glaciers were as much as one mile thick. As they moved south, the glaciers flattened the land, crushed boulders, and dug giant holes in the ground.

When the climate warmed, the ice melted. The holes filled with water and became Lake Ontario, Lake Erie, and the Finger Lakes of New York State. Now, many animals and plants live in these areas.

QUICK CHECK

Main Idea and Details **How were the Appalachian Mountains shaped?**

Plants and Animals of the Northeast

White Oak Tree

Mallard Duck

New England Aster

Blue Crab

Common Buttercup

Moose

B   A RICH LAND

The Northeastern coastline is dotted with **bays**. Bays are areas where the ocean is partly surrounded by land. This creates sheltered places called harbors, where ships can be safe from storms. Early settlers anchored their ships in these harbors. Over time, large cities including Baltimore, Maryland, and New York City, grew around these harbors.

Forests

At one time, forests carpeted the Northeast. They were a valuable resource for Native Americans and European settlers. Native Americans used tree trunks to build homes and carve canoes. European settlers used trees to build homes and ships. Both groups burned wood as **fuel**, something that produces energy.

Portland is the largest city in Maine.

Over time, many Northeastern forests were replaced by roads, farms, and towns, but trees are still an important resource in the region. The two main types of trees that grow in the Northeast are broadleaf trees, which lose their leaves each winter, and needle-leaf trees (also known as evergreens) which keep their leaves all year long. The maple is a broadleaf tree, and the spruce and pine are needle-leaf trees.

QUICK CHECK

Summarize Where did early settlers anchor their ships?

PLACES

Adirondack State Park is home to the largest "old growth" forest in the Northeast. An old growth forest is one in which the trees have never been cut down. Many animals, including black bears, live in old growth forests.

Black Bear in a Park

Spruce needles and cones

Maple leaf

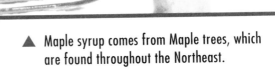

▲ Maple syrup comes from Maple trees, which are found throughout the Northeast.

137

ⓒ MOUNTAINS AND WATER

We've talked so far about forests and coastlines. Do you want to know what else is in the Northeast? Mountains, lots of them! Almost every Northeastern state has mountains. The Appalachian Mountains include smaller mountain ranges, such as the Green Mountains of Vermont and the Adirondack Mountains, which extend from Canada to New York.

There's a lot of water, too. Many rivers flow down these mountains. On the east side of the mountains, in areas where the land suddenly drops, then flattens into a plain, the flowing rivers turn into splashing waterfalls. Keep an eye out for these **fall lines** where land drops sharply to lower land below. You may see a waterfall!

Niagara Falls is a set of three separate waterfalls on the border between the United States and Canada.

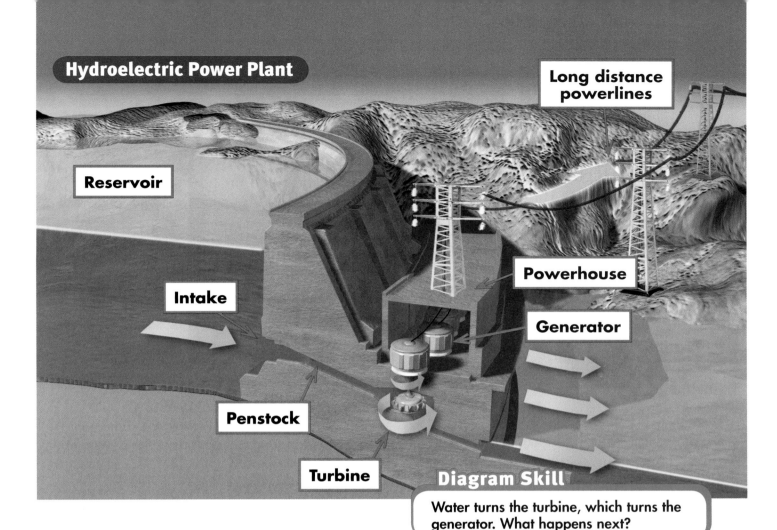

Hydroelectric Power Plant

Reservoir

Intake

Penstock

Turbine

Long distance powerlines

Powerhouse

Generator

Diagram Skill

Water turns the turbine, which turns the generator. What happens next?

All this water is used as a resource to produce energy for machines. Settlers used waterfalls to turn the wheels of their mills that ground grain. Water power is still used to run machines, such as those that create electricity.

The mountains and waters of the Northeast provide other resources, too. The mountains contain minerals such as coal. The region's bays and lakes, and of course the Atlantic Ocean, also offer resources—foods such as fish, crabs, and lobsters.

Cherrystone clams can be found along the coast of the Northeast. ▼

QUICK CHECK

Summarize **What are some resources found in the Northeast?**

ⓓ CLIMATE OF THE NORTHEAST

The Northeast has four seasons, but there are differences in the seasons within the region. At high elevations, such as the mountains of Maine, the climate is colder than in lower areas. In southern areas, such as coastal Maryland, the climate is warmer than in northern areas.

One thing all the states in the region share is precipitation in the form of snow and rain. The precipitation keeps the rivers full and forests and farmlands growing.

Much of the precipitation comes from storms that strike the region in the fall and winter. These are known as "nor'easters" (that's short for north-eastern). Lighthouses were built all along the northeastern coastline to help sailors see the land at night during storms and fog.

Fall Colors

In early fall, temperatures drop, and daylight hours shorten. These changes cause the green leaves of broadleaf trees to turn brilliant shades of orange, red, yellow, and brown. Many **tourists**, or people who travel to visit other places, travel to the Northeast each fall to see the colorful changing leaves.

QUICK CHECK

Compare and Contrast How is the climate in coastal Maryland different from the climate in the mountains of Maine?

Portland Head Light, a lighthouse near Portland, Maine, opened in 1791.

Check Understanding

1. **VOCABULARY** Write a sentence for each of the vocabulary words.

   glacier   fuel   fall line

2. **READING SKILL Main Idea and Details** Use the chart on page 134 to write about the geography of the Northeast.

Main Idea	Details

3. **Write About It** Write a paragraph about how European settlers' use of forests caused the region to change.

Map and Globe Skills

Compare Maps at Different Scales

VOCABULARY

map scale

small-scale map

large-scale map

Maps can't show places in the size they are on Earth. Instead, they use a **map scale** to tell you the actual size of an area on the map.

Map A is a **small-scale map**. It covers a large area, but can't include many details. Map B is a **large-scale map**. It shows many details of a smaller area.

Learn It

- Map A shows Maine. It shows a large area without many details. This is a small-scale map.

- Map B shows Acadia National Park on Maine's coast. It shows a smaller area with more details and information. It is a large-scale map.

Try It

- Which map shows the largest area?

- Using the scale on Map A, measure the distance from Seal Harbor to Swans Island. Do the same with Map B, using the scale on Map B. What did you find?

Apply It

- Compare a map of the United States with a map of your state. Which map is a small-scale map? Which is a large-scale map?

Map A: Maine

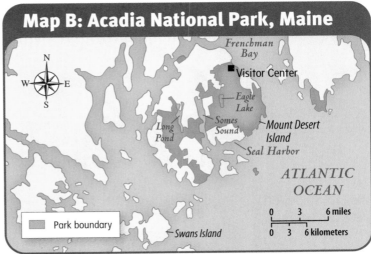

Map B: Acadia National Park, Maine

VOCABULARY

industry p. 145

service p. 146

urban p. 148

suburban p. 149

megalopolis p. 149

READING SKILL

Main Idea and Details
Copy the chart below.
As you read, fill it in with
information about working
in the Northeast.

Main Idea	Details

STANDARDS FOCUS

SOCIAL STUDIES Production, Distribution, and Consumption

GEOGRAPHY Environment and Society

The Economy of the Northeast

Cranberries are important to the economy of the Northeast.

Visual Preview

How have people of the Northeast adapted to make a living?

A Many people still earn a living in the Northeast by fishing and farming.

B People in the Northeast worked in manufacturing long ago.

C Many people in the Northeast work in service jobs.

D Most people in the Northeast live and work in cities and suburbs.

A USING RESOURCES

Most people in the Northeast live in or near cities. That's because manufacturing became an important part of the region's economy in the 1800s. Before that, most people depended on the natural resources in the region to make a living.

How do people in the Northeast make a living? Many people in the Northeast work in offices, but some people still make a living from the region's natural resources.

Along the coast from Maine to Maryland, fishing, trapping lobster and crabs, or digging for clams and oysters is still a full-time job. Further inland, people use the Northeast's rich land to earn a living. Each state in the region grows a wide variety of fruits and vegetables.

The Northeast's grassy areas provide food for cows. Dairy farmers use cow's milk to produce milk products, cheeses, and yogurt. Dairy farming is big business in Pennsylvania, New Jersey, Vermont, Connecticut, and New Hampshire. Look at the map to see where some of the items are grown.

Products of the Northeast

Trees, plants, flowers		Legumes	
Dairy		Maple syrup	
Fruit		Vegetables, Mushrooms	

Map Skill

LOCATION **In what states are fruits grown?**

QUICK CHECK

Main Idea and Details **What do the Northeast's grasslands do for its economy?**

B BUILDING FACTORIES

Did you know that people used to make almost everything they needed themselves? From hats to shoes and clothes to homes, if you needed it, you had to make it yourself. People even wove their own cloth.

In the late 1700s, some people in England discovered how to build machines that wove lots of cloth all at once. That meant people could buy cloth instead of making it.

Early Factories

In 1789 a man named Samuel Slater wrote the plans for one of these machines. He brought the plans to Rhode Island. Textile, or cloth, factories were soon being built all over the Northeast. Other businesses began to use the same ideas as

PEOPLE

In 1813, **Francis Lowell** built a textile factory in Massachusetts. The factory town built nearby was the first planned town for workers.

Francis Lowell

the textile factories to produce paper, tin, and other goods.

Many people left their homes to look for work at these new factories. Lucy Larcom began working in a Lowell textile mill when she was only 11. Lucy, like many young girls, worked to help support her family. Read what she had to say about her experience.

A town was built near the Lowell factory in Massachusetts so workers could live near the factory.

Mill

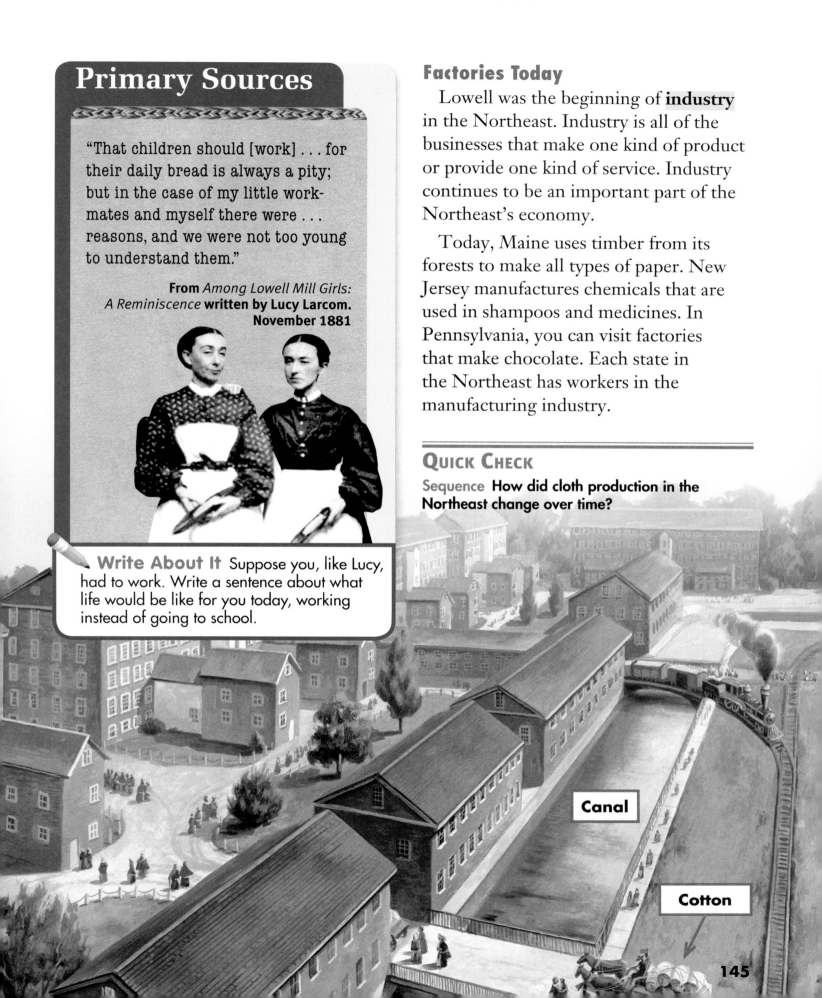

Primary Sources

"That children should [work] . . . for their daily bread is always a pity; but in the case of my little work-mates and myself there were . . . reasons, and we were not too young to understand them."

From *Among Lowell Mill Girls: A Reminiscence* **written by Lucy Larcom. November 1881**

Write About It Suppose you, like Lucy, had to work. Write a sentence about what life would be like for you today, working instead of going to school.

Factories Today

Lowell was the beginning of **industry** in the Northeast. Industry is all of the businesses that make one kind of product or provide one kind of service. Industry continues to be an important part of the Northeast's economy.

Today, Maine uses timber from its forests to make all types of paper. New Jersey manufactures chemicals that are used in shampoos and medicines. In Pennsylvania, you can visit factories that make chocolate. Each state in the Northeast has workers in the manufacturing industry.

QUICK CHECK

Sequence How did cloth production in the Northeast change over time?

Canal

Cotton

C   SERVING OTHERS

So far, you've read about the goods, or products, of the Northeast's agriculture and manufacturing industries. Many people in the Northeast don't produce goods or food. Instead, they provide a **service.** All the jobs that people do to help others are service jobs. As a matter of fact, many people in the United States provide services.

When you buy a snack at the local store, the person behind the counter provides a service. Your doctor and dentist also provide services when they help you keep your body and teeth healthy. Your teacher provides a service, too—he or she helps you learn new things.

Service Workers in the Northeast

People in Millions

3

2

1

0

Protective
Services

Retail and
Wholesale Trade

Restaurant

Jobs

What about when you go to a bike repair shop? The person who fixes your bike is providing a service, too. Throughout the region and the country, service workers provide services we can't or don't have the time to do ourselves.

Instead of having to make our own clothes and grow our own food as people did in the past, we rely on people who work in manufacturing and agriculture to provide these for us. All we need to do is to buy them from someone who works in a service job. Look at the chart below. Which two industries have about the same number of service workers?

QUICK CHECK

Summarize **What are some service jobs in the Northeast?**

Chart Skill

What industry has the most service providers in the Northeast?

Education   Healthcare   Other

147

D   CITIES AND SUBURBS

The Northeast has less land than any other region in the United States, but about one in every six people lives in the Northeast. Where do all the workers live?

Cities and Suburbs

The Northeast has a number of areas that are urban. Urban means "of the city"—in other words, all cities are urban centers.

The first big Northeast cities began as ports, or harbors, where ships landed with goods to trade. Trade with Europe was important to the early settlers and to the young United States. Eventually, these trading ports grew into cities. Later, the growing populations of city ports made them good places to build factories. Not only did they have a large supply of workers, but their location along harbors made it easy to ship goods to other places.

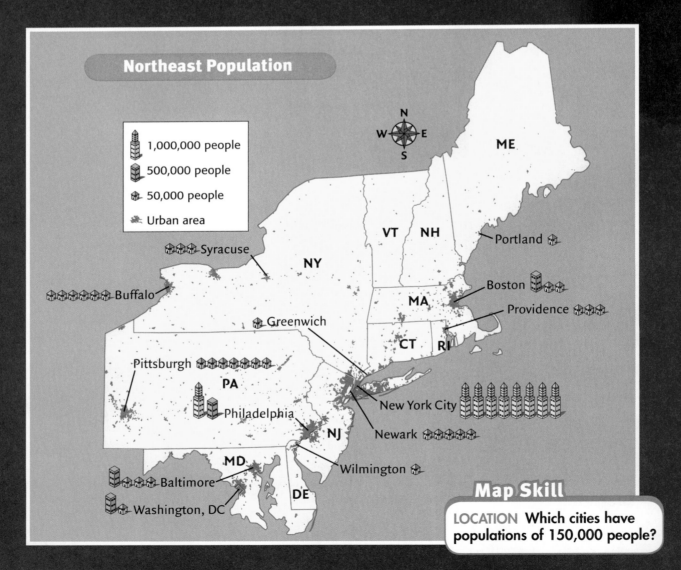

Northeast Population

- 1,000,000 people
- 500,000 people
- 50,000 people
- Urban area

Syracuse
Buffalo
Portland
Boston
Providence
Greenwich
Pittsburgh
Philadelphia
New York City
Newark
Wilmington
Baltimore
Washington, DC

ME, VT, NH, NY, MA, CT, RI, PA, NJ, MD, DE

Map Skill

LOCATION Which cities have populations of 150,000 people?

The Northeast's megalopolis is so big that it can be seen from space at night.

Today, many people in the Northeast live in suburban areas. A suburb is a community near a city. If you look closely, you can even see the word "urban" in suburban. Suburbs developed because people wanted to live in less crowded spaces, but near a city.

Bigger than a City

Together, a city and its suburbs form a metropolitan area. Some cities themselves are the suburbs of larger cities. For example, the city of Newark, New Jersey, is part of New York City's metropolitan area. A few Northeast metropolitan areas have grown so large they overlap. These overlapping metropolitan areas form a megalopolis—a single huge metropolitan area. One megalopolis runs from Boston to Washington, D.C.

QUICK CHECK

Summarize What did the first Northeast cities look like?

Check Understanding

1. **VOCABULARY** Write a paragraph about the economy of the Northeast using these words.

   urban   suburban   megalopolis

2. **READING SKILL** Main Idea and Details Use the chart from page 142 to write about the different types of factories in the Northeast.

Main Idea	Details

3. **Write About It** Write a sentence about how factories in the Northeast helped cause the region to grow.

149

VOCABULARY

culture p. 151

diverse p. 153

READING SKILL

Main Idea and Details
Copy the chart below.
As you read, fill it in with
information about people
of the Northeast.

Main Idea	Details

STANDARDS FOCUS

SOCIAL STUDIES — Culture

GEOGRAPHY — The Uses of Geography

The People of the Northeast

The Northeast is a diverse region.

Visual Preview

What is important to the culture of the Northeast?

A Native Americans are an important part of Northeast culture.

B Immigrants contribute to the rich diversity of the Northeast.

C Northeasterners hold festivals to celebrate their heritage.

D The Northeast has many activities to explore.

A MANY WAYS OF LIFE

For hundreds of years, people from all over the world have settled in the Northeast. These immigrants brought their ways of life with them and helped to enrich the region.

What does your family do during holidays? What language do you speak at home? What foods do you eat? All of this and more is part of your **culture**. Culture includes a people's history, language, religion, and customs, or ways of doing things. It also includes a people's stories, songs, and jokes.

The cultures that came to the Northeast were a rich mix. Each culture brought its foods, ways of having fun, and styles of music and art. This joining of cultures has shaped life in the Northeast region.

First Northeasterners

The first people in the Northeast were Native Americans. The Iroquois and the Lenape are two of the many Native American groups in the region. They grew maize, beans, and squash for food. They also ate wild plants. The Iroquois knew about maple syrup and tapped maple trees to get the syrup. Native Americans also hunted deer and other wild animals. They used deer hides to make their clothing.

QUICK CHECK

Main Idea and Details **Describe Native Americans of the Northeast.**

Many Chinese immigrants came to the United States in the 1800s. ▼

▲ Irish immigrants have greatly influenced the Northeast. This Irish family arrived in New York in 1929.

B IMMIGRANTS THEN AND NOW

In the early 1600s, Native Americans encountered people who had sailed from England. These settlers came for a better life.

Settlers came from the Netherlands and Sweden, too. Johan Printz, the leader of a Swedish settlement in Pennsylvania, had this to say about the New World:

This is a very lovely country with everything a person can wish himself on this earth.

JOHAN PRINTZ

Soon, more and more people came to settle in what they called the "New World." These new settlers slowly pushed out most of the Native Americans who had lived in the area. By 1750, the English had settled in colonies throughout the region. Eventually, other Europeans found homes in the Northeast. People from Sweden moved to Delaware, while New York was settled by people from the Netherlands. Many Germans made their homes in Pennsylvania.

Africans were another important group of people to arrive in the 1600s. Most came against their will as enslaved workers, but some Africans came as servants who would be free men and women after a period of time.

▲ People of Hispanic origin are a large part of the rich cultural heritage of the Northeast.

Many Africans, like this Ethiopian family, are enriching the Northeast's cultural diversity. ▼

EVENT

The **Amish left Europe** in the early 1700s in search of religious freedom. They first settled in Pennsylvania. Today there are Amish communities in 22 states around the country.

Amish School Boys

Ellis Island and People Today

As the Northeast grew, its people became more diverse. Diverse means that there is a variety.

From about 1892 to 1954, immigrants from around the world came to the Northeast and stopped at Ellis Island in New York City's harbor.

There, officials tried to make sure that only healthy people entered the United States.

In recent years, people from China and other Asian nations have moved to the Northeast. Others have come from Mexico and the Dominican Republic.

Wherever they came from, people arrived in the Northeast looking for a better life and a better future. They brought with them their culture and ideas and shared them with others.

QUICK CHECK

Summarize Why did many immigrant groups come to the Northeast?

153

C   CELEBRATING CULTURES

People in the Northeast are proud of the many cultures that make up their region. One way to show pride in your culture is by sharing it with others. Many groups do this by having festivals. These festivals are full of tasty foods, music, and lively dancing.

Festivals For Everyone

One of the of the largest celebrations is Saint Patrick's Day. Irish Americans celebrate the day by attending one of the many parades in the region. Towns with large German-American populations celebrate the fall harvest during Oktoberfest. At Oktoberfest, people eat bratwurst, a type of sausage, and dance to music played on an accordion.

EVENT

Every year, Philadelphia, Pennsylvania, hosts **the Mummers Parade** on New Year's Day. The parade grew out of European customs brought to the city by early settlers.

Mummers Parade

Other cultural groups hold festivals, too. Poughkeepsie, New York, holds a Greek festival with dancing and Greek foods, such as spanakopita, a spinach and feta cheese pie. Each spring, a Japanese festival called Sakura Matsuri, part of the National Cherry Blossom Festival, is held in Washington, D.C. Visitors can taste Japanese food and learn the Japanese art of paper folding, or origami. On Labor Day weekend, Scranton, Pennsylvania, holds La Festa Italiana. This is a celebration of Italian culture, music, and food.

Japanese musicians perform during the National Cherry Blossom Festival. ▼

QUICK CHECK

Draw conclusions **Why do cultural groups in the Northeast hold celebrations?**

Global Connections

New York City's Caribbean Festival

One of the world's largest festivals happens each Labor Day weekend in Brooklyn, New York. It's the West Indian American Day Carnival and Parade.

The popular festival celebrates the cultures of the West Indies. These islands in the Caribbean Sea include Jamaica, Trinidad and Tobago, St. Kitts, and Barbados, among others. Many people in the Northeast were born in the West Indies or have parents or grandparents who were. At the festival, they and others can enjoy the dances, music, art, and food of the West Indies.

The festival begins at two in the morning with a parade. Festival-goers wear costumes and walk through the streets of New York City to the music of steel drums. Later in the day, people enjoy foods such as fried fish, coconut bread, and a leafy vegetable called callaloo.

Brooklyn, NY

Dancers wear elaborate costumes during the West Indian Day Parade. ▼

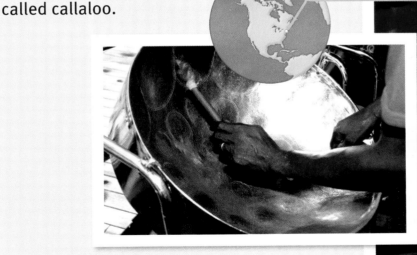

▲ People play steel drums during the West Indian Day parade.

155

Citizenship
Working for the Common Good

What are some ways that kids can work for the common good? Some students in New York decided to get involved in a project that would make their neighborhood more beautiful. They found an organization that would help them make positive changes in their environment by creating open spaces with trees and flowers. These kids helped to create an open garden where anyone could gather.

Write About It Write about how you could work for the common good.

You've read about the diverse cultures of the people of the Northeast and about their celebrations. The region is also full of places to visit.

If you like the outdoors, it's a fantastic place to be. You can hike in the mountains or sail along the region's coast.

Perhaps you enjoy seeing exhibits at museums. You can talk to dolphin trainers at the National Aquarium in Baltimore, Maryland, or view fine art at many museums in the region. If you want to see a replica of America's first submarine, "the Turtle," head to the United States Navy's Submarine Force Museum in Groton, Connecticut.

Sailboats race on Lake Champlain in Vermont.

This family watches a large shark at the National Aquarium in Baltimore, Maryland.

Culture and Environment

For music, you can go to Tanglewood in Lenox, Massachusetts. It's the summer home of the Boston Symphony Orchestra. One musician who has played at Tanglewood is Yo Yo Ma, a cellist. Like many Northeasterners, Yo Yo Ma is interested in learning how the world's cultures have mixed to create beautiful music.

People in the Northeast enjoy their environment so much that many work to keep it clean and healthy. Read p.156 to see how some kids worked for the common good of the Northeast.

QUICK CHECK

Summarize What are some of the things that people in the Northeast can do for fun?

Check Understanding

1. **VOCABULARY** Write a sentence that uses each of these vocabulary words.

   culture   **diverse**

2. **READING SKILL Main Idea and Details** Use the chart from page 150 to write about places to explore in the Northeast.

Main Idea	Details

EXPLORE The Big Idea

3. **Write About It** Write a paragraph about how the population of the Northeast has changed over time.

Review and Assess

Vocabulary

Copy the sentences below. Use the list of vocabulary words to fill in the blanks.

glacier   megalopolis

fall line   cultures

1. The _____ is where mountains flatten into a plain.

2. Two or more metropolitan areas that overlap form a _____.

3. A _____ is a moving sheet of ice.

4. The people of the Northeast come from many different _____.

Comprehension and Critical Thinking

5. What is the difference between broadleaf and needle-leaf trees?

6. What kinds of resources can be found in the Northeast?

7. **Critical Thinking** Why were cities built near harbors?

8. **Reading Skill** What places in the Northeast would you most enjoy visiting? Explain why using the main idea and details.

Skill

Compare Maps at Different Scales

9. What is the difference between a large-scale map and a small-scale map?

10. Look at the maps on this page. Which map is a large-scale map?

Ellis Island, New York

Northeast United States

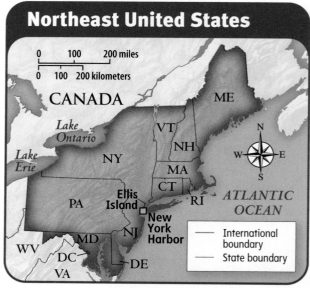

Test Preparation

Read the paragraphs. Then answer the questions.

New Hampshire's newest state forest . . . was purchased by The Nature Conservancy . . . . It . . . will never be developed . . . It will always be open. . . . [and] it provides an ideal habitat for an endangered plant species called the northeastern bulrush.

This is good news. Teachers use the land for forestry, science, and other subjects. Students tap trees, while environmental science students measure the effects of ozone pollution on white pine. Gym classes go snow-shoeing and hiking in the forest, and the schools' cross-country ski team trains on its trails.

1. What is the main idea of the passage?

A. New Hampshire has beautiful forests.

B. Teachers use land for forestry and science.

C. The Nature Conservancy bought the forest to provide a habitat for the northeastern bulrush.

D. The state forest will provide habitat for an endangered species and provide students a place to learn.

2. Why is it important to have undeveloped land? What does it provide the community?

3. Which of the following statements is an opinion?

A. The northeastern bulrush is an endangered plant species.

B . The Nature Conservancy is the newest state forest in New Hampshire.

C. The Nature Conservancy bought the newest state forest.

D. New Hampshire has beautiful state forests.

4. List reasons why it is important to provide habitat for plants and animals that are endangered.

The Big Idea Activities

What causes a region to change?

Write About the Big Idea

Expository Report

Recall what you learned about the geography, economy, and people of the Northeast in Unit 3. Review your notes in the completed foldable.

Use the information from your foldable and other sources to write a report. Your report should end up being several paragraphs. The topic of your report will explain what caused the Northeast to change over time.

FOLDABLES
Study Organizer

People
Economy
Geography
The Northeast

Plan a Bike Trip

Suppose you are a travel agent. Your newest client wants you to plan a bike trip. Work with a partner to plan a trip through part of the Northeast.

1. Research areas of the Northeast that might be best suited to a bike trip.

2. Use a map to figure out the best routes.

3. Create a presentation for your client. It should include pictures and descriptions, and even a map, of the trip you are suggesting.

4. You may draw pictures or create a collage from newspapers or magazines.

5. Present your trip to your class. Be sure to explain why you chose the particular route you selected.

EXPLORE The Big Idea

Essential Question
How do people affect the environment?

FOLDABLES
Study Organizer

Summarize
Use a three-tab book foldable to take notes as you read Unit 4. Label the three tabs **Geography of the Southeast**, **Economy of the Southeast**, and **People of the Southeast**.

Geography of the Southeast | Economy of the Southeast | People of the Southeast

LOG ON

For more about Unit 4 go to
www.macmillanmh.com

The Southeast

PEOPLE, PLACES, and EVENTS

Sequoyah

Sequoyah Birthplace Museum

Sequoyah was a Cherokee silversmith who lived in Tennessee. He spent 12 years creating an alphabet that allowed the Cherokee to write their language for the first time.

Today you can visit the **Sequoyah Birthplace Museum** in Vonore, Tennessee.

Wynton Marsalis

New Orleans Jazz and Heritage Festival

Wynton Marsalis began his career in New Orleans and is now a famous jazz trumpet player.

Today you can hear many famous musicians play at the **New Orleans Jazz and Heritage Festival**.

For more about People, Places, and Events, visit:
www.macmillanmh.com

Selma, Alabama

Voting Rights

Citizens from all over the United States protested the unfair treatment of African Americans by walking in a march from **Selma, Alabama,** to Montgomery, Alabama and supporting **voting rights for** African Americans.

Today you can walk the National Historic Trail that follows the path protesters walked between Selma and Montgomery.

Pony Penning

Barrier Islands

Barrier islands form when ocean waves deposit sand along a coast. Assateague Island, one of the most famous of the barrier islands in the Southeast, is known for its population of wild horses.

Today at the annual **Pony Penning**, you can watch the horses swim to the mainland where the young horses are sold.

Southeast Region

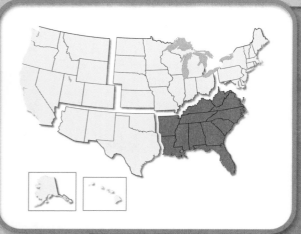

1 Country music often includes fiddles. Nashville, Tennessee, is home to the Country Music Hall of Fame and Museum.

People enjoy all sorts of outdoor activities in the warm Southeast.

OZARK PLATEAU

Arkansas River

AR

★Little Rock

OUACHITA MOUNTAINS

Mississippi Ri.

Vicksburg National Millitary Park

Red River

Jackso

LA

Baton Rouge ★

G U L

5

Lacassine National Wildlife Refuge

6 The White Magnolia is the state flower of both Mississippi and Louisiana.

5 The Mississippi is one of the longest rivers in the United States. Steamboats like this one carry tourists up and down the river.

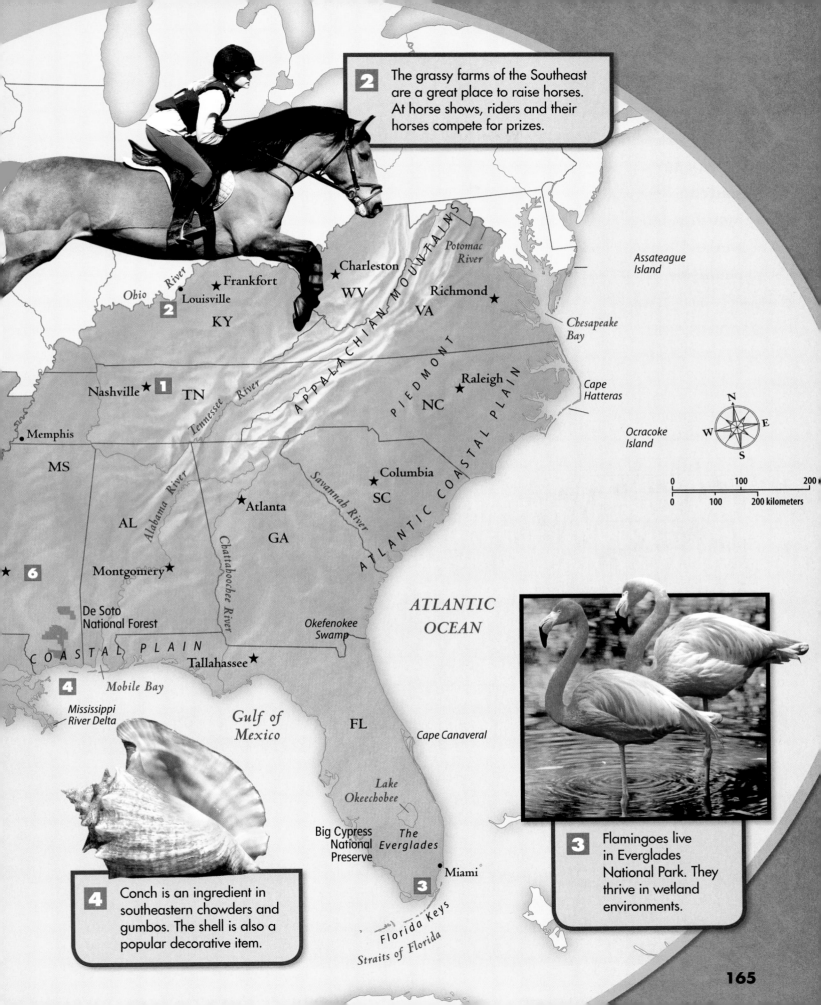

2 The grassy farms of the Southeast are a great place to raise horses. At horse shows, riders and their horses compete for prizes.

Assateague Island

Potomac River

Charleston

Frankfort ★

Ohio River

Louisville

2

KY

WV

Richmond ★

VA

Chesapeake Bay

APPALACHIAN MOUNTAINS

Nashville ★ **1**

TN

Tennessee River

PIEDMONT

Raleigh ★

NC

Cape Hatteras

Memphis

MS

Ocracoke Island

N
W   E
S

Columbia ★

SC

ATLANTIC COASTAL PLAIN

Savannah River

0   100   200 miles

0   100   200 kilometers

AL

Atlanta ★

GA

Alabama River

Montgomery ★

6

Chattahoochee River

De Soto National Forest

Okefenokee Swamp

ATLANTIC OCEAN

COASTAL PLAIN

4

Tallahassee ★

Mobile Bay

Mississippi River Delta

Gulf of Mexico

FL

Cape Canaveral

Lake Okeechobee

Big Cypress National Preserve

The Everglades

3

Miami

Florida Keys

Straits of Florida

4 Conch is an ingredient in southeastern chowders and gumbos. The shell is also a popular decorative item.

3 Flamingoes live in Everglades National Park. They thrive in wetland environments.

165

Lesson 1

VOCABULARY

source p. 167

mouth p. 167

wetland p. 167

peninsula p. 168

levee p. 172

READING SKILL

Summarize

Copy the chart . Fill it in with details about the geography of the Southeast.

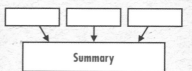

Summary

STANDARDS FOCUS

SOCIAL STUDIES People, Places and Environments

GEOGRAPHY Physical Systems

The Geography of the Southeast

Visual Preview

How does the Southeast's geography affect the region?

A The Southeast has many water-loving animals in its rivers and wetlands.

B Islands form in different ways.

C Some parts of the Southeast are hit by big storms.

D Walls are built along rivers in the Southeast to help prevent flooding.

Ⓐ RIVERS AND WETLANDS

The Southeast has a little of everything—mountains, rolling hills, a broad coastal plain, and many islands. Most of all, the region has plenty of water!

The Mississippi River is the second longest river in North America. It runs 2,350 miles from its **source**, or beginning, in Minnesota to its **mouth**, or end, at the Gulf of Mexico in Louisiana.

A Region of Wetlands

Much of the Southeast is low, flat land. When rain falls, it does not always drain away. As a result, the Southeast has a lot of **wetlands**, or areas where water is always on or close to the surface of the ground.

In the past, people often drained wetlands so they could build on the land. Now we know that wetlands are valuable. They act like giant

PLACES

The **Okefenokee Swamp** covers more than 430,000 acres in Georgia. You can take a boat tour, but watch out for alligators!

Okefenokee Swamp

sponges that help control floods. Wetlands also act as filters. As water flows through them, the wetland soils remove pollution from the water. Many plants and animals live in the wetlands of the Southeast.

QUICK CHECK

Summarize **How are wetlands valuable?**

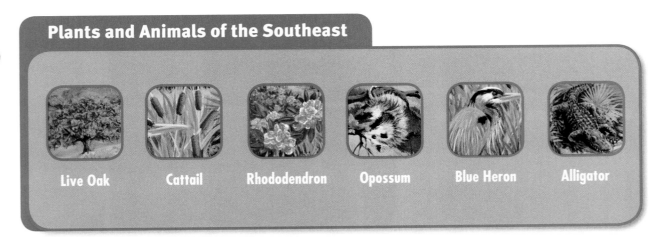

Plants and Animals of the Southeast

Live Oak   Cattail   Rhododendron   Opossum   Blue Heron   Alligator

B LANDFORMS IN THE SOUTHEAST

Look at the map on pages 164-165. Which bodies of water border the Southeast states? You can see that the Southeast has miles of coastline. The land along the coast is low and flat. In some places, this flatland stretches for many miles inland. The land is rich and good for farming.

Find Florida on the map. Florida is a **peninsula**, or an area of land that is surrounded by water on three sides.

Hills and Mountains

As you move inland from the coast, you come to gently rolling hills. These hills are called the Piedmont, or foothills.

Next are the Appalachian Mountains. These mountains have been worn down by erosion over millions of years. They are not as high as mountains that formed more recently. At 6,684 feet, Mount Mitchell in North Carolina is the highest peak in the Appalachian Mountains. The Appalachian Mountains run through the Northeast and Southeast. Which states do they run through in the Southeast?

Islands

The Southeast also has plenty of islands. Did you know that islands can be formed in different ways? You can read about how three different islands were formed in the chart below.

QUICK CHECK

Summarize **What are the landforms in the Southeast?**

Islands in the Southeast

Figure Eight Island, North Carolina

Barrier islands form as ocean waves drop tons of sand along the coast. They act like barriers, or walls, to protect the mainland from the ocean waves.

Key West, Florida

The Florida Keys are made from the bones of coral, a tiny sea animal. As the coral grows together, it may rise above the ocean's surface.

Puerto Rico

The island of Puerto Rico formed about 190 million years ago when underground rocks were pushed together and forced upwards.

Chart Skill

Which island was made by waves dropping sand along a coast?

These horses live on a farm in the Appalachian Mountains in West Virginia.

C THE CLIMATE OF THE SOUTHEAST

If you like warm weather, you'll love the Southeast. Most of the Southeast has a climate of warm or hot summers and mild winters. Near the Gulf of Mexico, the climate is usually warm and humid. Humid air holds lots of moisture.

During the day, sunlight warms both water in the Gulf of Mexico and nearby land. Sunlight warms land faster than it warms water. As the ground warms, it heats the air above it. The warm air rises, and cooler air from over the water moves to replace it. A sea breeze blows from the water toward the land.

As night falls, land cools faster than water. Warm air rises over the water. Cooler air from over the land moves to replace it. A land breeze blows from the land towards the water.

The Gulf of Mexico affects the climate by cooling the land in summer and warming it in winter. In the summer, water stays cooler longer than land does, so cool breezes blow off the Gulf onto the nearby land. In winter, the water is warmer than the land, so the breezes from the water onto the land bring warm air.

Air Movement in Sea and Land Breezes

sea breeze, day

land breeze, night

KEY

→ warm air

→ cold air

In the northern part of the Southeast region, especially in the Appalachian Mountains, it is usually cooler than in the deep South. In winter, there may even be some snow in the mountains of West Virginia, Tennessee, and North Carolina—but it never lasts for long.

The entire region gets rain, but there are also sunny days. In fact, Florida's nickname is the "Sunshine State."

Storm Season

Sometimes the weather in the Southeast is not so pleasant. Coastal areas in the Southeast may be hit by hurricanes in the late summer and fall. Hurricane winds and waves may cause floods and damage buildings and trees.

QUICK CHECK

Summarize **What is the climate of the Southeast?**

▲ Hurricane Katrina was the third-strongest hurricane that has ever hit the United States.

These brown pelicans live along the Florida coast.

Since much of the Southeast is low land, heavy rains can cause floods. To prevent floods, people have built **levees**, or large walls, along the shores of some rivers to keep the rivers from overflowing.

Hurricane Damage

Hurricane Katrina hit land near New Orleans, Louisiana, in 2005. Levees that held back water from a nearby lake were broken. Water rushed in and flooded part of the city. Some people lost their lives, and many people lost their homes. The hurricane's winds also did millions of dollars worth of damage to towns along the Mississippi and Alabama coasts.

Levees along the Mississippi River in Louisiana prevent flooding. ▼

levee

Scientists worry that there may be more and stronger hurricanes in the future, because the world's climate seems to be getting warmer. Engineers and scientists keep looking for ways to prevent future storms from causing so much damage.

QUICK CHECK

Make Inferences **What damage may happen when rivers overflow?**

Check Understanding

1. **VOCABULARY** Write a postcard to a friend that uses the following vocabulary words.

   source   mouth   levee

2. **READING SKILL** Summarize Use the chart from page 166 to write about the geography of the Southeast.

3. **Write About It** Write a paragraph about what the people in the Southeast have done to prevent flooding.

Chart and Graph Skills

Read Circle Graphs

VOCABULARY
graph
circle graph

A **graph** is a drawing that helps you compare information by showing the relationship between things. The graph shown here is a **circle graph**. Circle graphs show how parts of something fit into the whole. Because each part looks like a slice of pie, a circle graph is sometimes called a pie graph.

Learn It

- The title of the graph tells you what is shown in the graph. This circle graph shows the U.S. states that produce the most grapefruit.

- The labels tell you what each slice represents. You can see that the yellow slice stands for the percentage of grapefruit that is grown in Texas.

- A larger slice means more grapefruit is grown in that state.

Leading U.S. States in the Production of Grapefruit

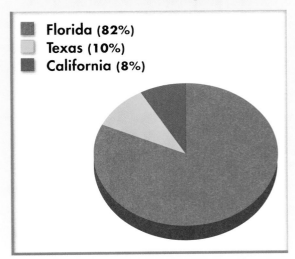

- Florida (82%)
- Texas (10%)
- California (8%)

Try It

- Compare the slices. Which state grows the most grapefruit?

- Which state grows more grapefruit—California or Texas?

- Which state grows the least grapefruit?

Apply It

- Make a circle graph that shows how much time you spend on each of the following activities during one day: sleeping, eating, school, watching TV, playing sports, doing homework, and other activities.

173

The Economy of the Southeast

VOCABULARY

renewable resource p. 176

petroleum p. 176

refinery p. 176

nonrenewable resource p. 177

READING SKILL

Summarize
Copy the chart below. As you read, fill it in with information about the economy of the Southeast.

Summary

STANDARDS FOCUS

SOCIAL STUDIES — Production, Distribution, and Consumption

GEOGRAPHY — Environment and Society

The Southeast has rich natural resources of farmland, forests, and minerals.

Visual Preview

How have people affected the economy of the Southeast?

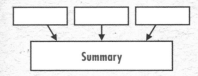

A Crops such as cotton and timber are grown on farms in the Southeast.

B Coal is one of the mineral resources in the Southeast.

C Factories in the Southeast make many products.

D In the Southeast, many people work in the service industry.

A   A RICH LAND

What do you need for farming? Rich soil, plenty of rain, and sunlight are important. The Southeast has all of these, along with short, mild winters.

When the first settlers from Europe came to the Southeast, they began to grow crops. The first crops were indigo (a plant used to make a dark blue dye) and tobacco. Later they began to grow rice and cotton. By the middle of the 1800s, cotton was the most important crop grown in the Southeast. It was sold to factories in Great Britain and in the Northeast.

Farm Products Today

Cotton is not as important to the Southeast's economy today. Almost every state in the Southeast, however, still grows some cotton.

For centuries, tobacco was a crop that American colonists in the Southeast could sell. Due to health concerns, fewer people today smoke cigarettes. As a result, there's less demand for tobacco. Farmers in these states are now growing other crops. North Carolina is known for growing sweet potatoes, Georgia for peaches and pecans, and Florida for oranges.

QUICK CHECK

Summarize **What crops are grown in the Southeast today?**

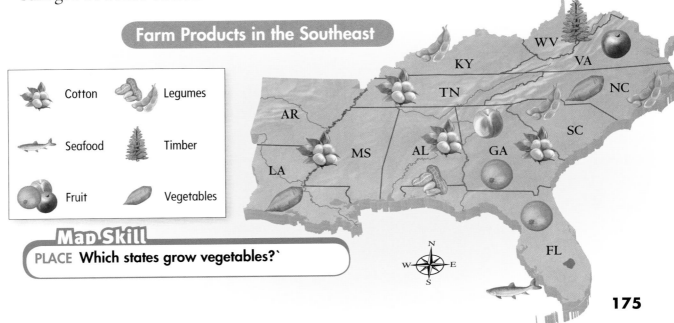

Farm Products in the Southeast

- Cotton
- Seafood
- Fruit
- Legumes
- Timber
- Vegetables

WV, KY, VA, TN, NC, AR, SC, MS, AL, GA, LA, FL

Map Skill
PLACE **Which states grow vegetables?**

B NATURAL RESOURCES

In addition to its rich soil and good climate, the Southeast has other natural resources that include trees, oil, and coal. As trees are cut down and used for lumber, they can be replaced by planting new trees. Natural materials that can be replaced are called **renewable resources**.

Other resources, such as coal, are found underground. People have been burning coal as fuel for thousands of years. Most of the coal mined in the United States is used to run power plants that make electricity.

Petroleum, or oil, is another important underground resource. To reach oil, workers drill deep into the ground. The oil is pumped to the surface, where it is shipped to oil **refineries**. A refinery is a factory that turns the oil into useful products such as gasoline and heating oil.

This coal mine in West Virginia is a strip mine. ▼

Problems with Natural Resources

Coal and oil are both **nonrenewable resources**, or natural materials that can't be replaced. Both took millions of years to form. Once the coal or oil is used up, it is gone forever. However, we are not going to run out of coal soon. We have enough to last about 250 years.

Burning coal to run power plants puts pollution into the air, including a gas called carbon dioxide. Many scientists think that too much of this gas in the air is causing the world's climate to get warmer.

Another problem with coal is the way it is mined. In the past, mines were deep underground. Today coal companies find strip mining easier and cheaper. You can see, by looking at the diagram below, how strip mining destroys forests and changes the land. Whether coal is worth the problems it causes is something people must decide.

QUICK CHECK

Compare and Contrast **How are renewable and nonrenewable resources different?**

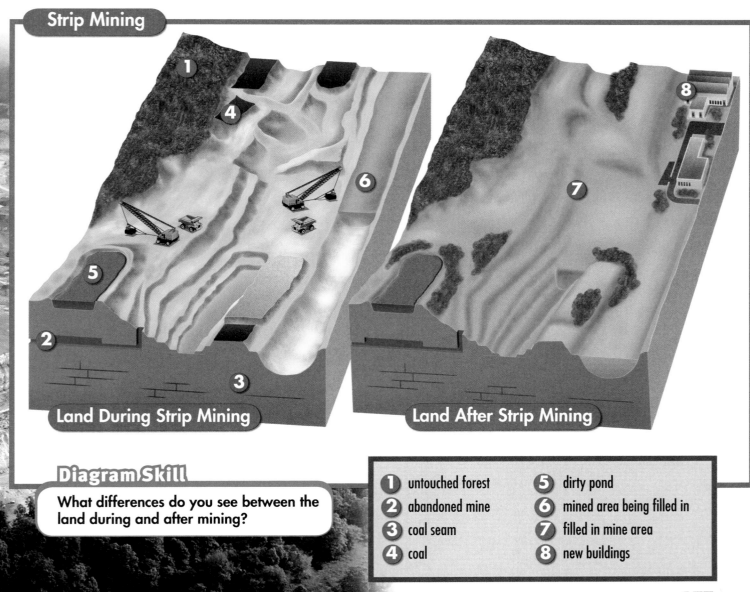

Strip Mining

Land During Strip Mining

Land After Strip Mining

Diagram Skill

What differences do you see between the land during and after mining?

① untouched forest		⑤ dirty pond	
② abandoned mine		⑥ mined area being filled in	
③ coal seam		⑦ filled in mine area	
④ coal		⑧ new buildings	

▲ Furniture is made throughout the Southeast.

▲ A factory worker checks a truck in this manufacturing plant.

ⓒ MANUFACTURING AND TECHNOLOGY

Are you wearing a shirt made of cotton? Perhaps the cotton was grown and the cloth was made in the Southeast. For many years, textile manufacturing was an important industry, especially in North Carolina. Currently, more and more textiles are being made in other countries.

As textiles have become less important to the Southeast's economy, electronics and the computer industry have become larger industries. Today factories in the Southeast manufacture paper, furniture, chemicals, cars, and soft drinks. These factories provide employment for many people.

EVENT

On May 5, 1961, astronaut Alan B. Shepard became the first American to enter space. His **15-minute flight on the Mercury 3** space capsule was launched from Cape Canaveral, Florida.

Mercury 3

DataGraphic
Jobs in the Southeast

The circle graph shows the number of people employed in each kind of industry in the Southeast. The bar graph shows the percent of service jobs for each Southeast state. Both graphs show that over fifty percent of the jobs in the Southeast are service jobs.

Employment in the Southeast

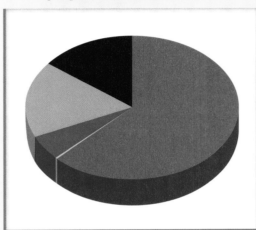

- Service Jobs
- Farming, Fishing, Forestry
- Construction
- Production, Transportation
- Other

Service Jobs in the Southeast

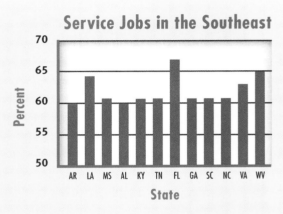

Talk About It

1. Are more people in the Southeast employed in construction or in production and transportation?

2. Which state has the largest percentage of workers in the service industry?

3. Which industry in the Southeast employs the most people?

Technology

Technology research is another important part of the Southeast's economy. Much of this research takes place at universities near Raleigh and Durham in North Carolina. Scientists there study everything from dinosaur eggs to the Mars space flights. Florida and Alabama also have important centers for space research.

QUICK CHECK

Main Idea and Details What are some products made in the Southeast?

While tourists are enjoying the beaches in the Southeast, they need services that include food, housing, transportation, and renting sports equipment.

D SERVING PEOPLE

Do you know what a snowbird is? It's a type of bird, but it is also a nickname for people who live in the North during the summer and in the South during winter. Some "snowbirds" stay in the South for the whole winter while others visit for only a short time. In recent years, many people have moved to the Southeast to live year-round.

Each year millions of snowbirds and other tourists visit the Southeast. They enjoy the beaches, national parks, theme parks, and famous places such as Colonial Williamsburg in Virginia. Florida alone attracts about 40 million tourists a year.

Serving Visitors

Of course, serving these visitors creates thousands of jobs. Some people work at attractions and theme parks, while other people work in hotels, restaurants, ground and air transportation, and all the other businesses that vacationers need.

QUICK CHECK

Make Generalizations **Why is the Southeast a popular place to visit in the winter?**

Check Understanding

1. **VOCABULARY** Make a brochure that explains the difference between the following vocabulary words.

   renewable resource

   nonrenewable resource

2. **READING SKILL** Summarize Use the chart from page 174 to write a paragraph about the natural resources of the Southeast.

3. **Write About It** Write a paragraph about how mining for coal has changed the environment of the Southeast.

VOCABULARY

dialect p. 185

segregation p. 186

READING SKILL

Summarize
Copy the chart. Fill it in about the people of the Southeast.

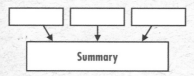

Summary

STANDARDS FOCUS

SOCIAL STUDIES — Culture

GEOGRAPHY — The Uses of Geography

The People of the Southeast

A parade float travels through a crowd in New Orleans, Louisiana.

Visual Preview

How do people of the Southeast shape the region's culture?

A The Cherokee and other Native Americans live in the Southeast.

B People from around the world came to the Southeast.

C The civil rights movement brought many changes to the Southeast.

D Music is an important part of the Southeast's culture.

Ⓐ NATIVE AMERICANS

The first people to live in the Southeast were Native Americans, including the Choctaw, Creek, Seminole, and Cherokee. They grew tobacco and "the three sisters"—corn, beans, and squash.

The Cherokee were one of the largest groups of Native Americans. Their lands stretched from Ohio to Alabama. Sequoyah was a Cherokee leader. He invented a way to write the Cherokee language.

Trail of Tears

In the 1830s, the United States government forced the Cherokee off their lands so that European settlers could live there. The Cherokee were forced to walk hundreds of miles to what is now Oklahoma. The journey they made was called the Trail of Tears, because so many Cherokee died on the way due to illness, hunger, or exhaustion.

Today, the Cherokee live in many places in the United States, including the Southeast. You can visit Oconaluftee Village in North Carolina to see how a typical Cherokee village would have looked 250 years ago.

PEOPLE

Sequoyah used letters from English, Greek, and Hebrew to make a system of 85 symbols that represented all the sounds in the Cherokee language.

Sequoyah

The Cherokee make beautiful beadwork, clay pots, and grass baskets.

QUICK CHECK

Summarize Why were the Cherokee forced off their lands?

183

Have you ever visited St. Augustine, Florida? It was settled by Spanish explorers in 1565. That makes it the oldest continuously lived-in European settlement in this country. Besides Florida, the Spanish explored other parts of the Southeast.

English explorers also came to America. In 1607 they built a colony in Jamestown, Virginia. They eventually built more colonies along the Atlantic Coast. The English colonists learned how to grow tobacco from Native Americans in the area. Later, people from Ireland and Scotland settled in the Appalachian Mountains of Virginia and North and South Carolina. They brought their songs and music, which you can still hear today.

Africans are another group of people whose culture, music, and food are part of the Southeast. Many Africans came to the region unwillingly. Most had been kidnapped and enslaved. They were forced to work on farms in the South.

French Settlers in the Southeast

Some French people settled in Louisiana. Others settled a colony in Canada called Acadia. When the British forced the Acadians out of Canada, many of them fled to Louisiana. Their descendants today are known as Cajuns.

The language, customs, and food of all of these cultures became part of the culture of the Southeast. Gumbo, a popular food in the Southeast, is a blend of ingredients from different cultures. You can read below what writer John T. Edge says about Southern food.

QUICK CHECK

Summarize **Which immigrant groups came to the Southeast?**

French culture is still seen in Louisiana, especially in New Orleans, where many people speak a **dialect** of French. A dialect is a form of a language spoken in a certain place by a certain group of people. One dialect is called Louisiana Creole.

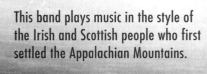

This band plays music in the style of the Irish and Scottish people who first settled the Appalachian Mountains.

Primary Sources

"Food tells us who we are, tells us something about our social, political, and economic ways . . . Food is one of the great shared creations of the South."

John T. Edge

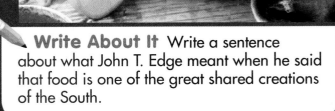

Write About It Write a sentence about what John T. Edge meant when he said that food is one of the great shared creations of the South.

Supporters of the civil rights movement held a sit-in at a lunch counter in Greensboro, North Carolina.

ⓒ CHANGING TIMES

The American Civil War in the 1860s brought an end to slavery. Changes to the United States Constitution made former enslaved peoples citizens and gave them rights. African Americans still faced unfair treatment and discrimination.

Segregation, or the practice of keeping racial groups separate, was a part of daily life in America. This meant that African American children attended different schools from white children. It also meant that African Americans were not allowed to eat in the same restaurants, ride in the same railway cars, stay at the same hotels, or join the same clubs as white people.

In the late 1950s and 1960s, people began working to give all Americans equal rights. This became known as the civil rights movement. Martin Luther King, Jr., Ralph Abernathy, and Rosa Parks were leaders in this movement. African Americans and other supporters of the civil rights movement held many peaceful protests and marches.

Every American citizen must have an equal right to vote.

—LYNDON BAINES JOHNSON

Young people played an important role in the movement. In 1957 nine African American students started attending a high school in Arkansas that had previously had only white students. In North Carolina and Tennessee, African American college students protested by holding "sit-ins." They would sit at a segregated lunch counter until they were served or until the store closed.

The Civil Rights Movement was successful. In 1964 and 1965, President Lyndon Johnson signed two new laws that protected the rights of all Americans. The Civil Rights Act of 1964 made it illegal to treat people differently because of their race, origin, religion, or gender. The next year, the Voting Rights Act of 1965 was passed. This law outlawed practices, like special taxes and tests, that had been used to prevent African Americans from voting.

Celebrating Freedom

In many places in the Southeast, African Americans hold a festival every year on June 19th. These "Juneteenth" festivals celebrate the day the end of slavery was announced in Galveston, Texas.

QUICK CHECK

Main Idea and Details **What was the civil rights movement?**

Citizenship

Being Informed

Lois heard that some towns celebrate a festival called Juneteenth every June 19th. She decided to find out more about it. She learned that "Juneteenth" celebrates the day that many enslaved people learned they were free. Today Juneteenth celebrations include African dancers and drummers, drama, storytelling, and great food. Lois decided to write to her town board to see if her town could start a Juneteenth celebration, too.

Write About It Write a paragraph about a festival that is celebrated in your town.

D A CELEBRATION OF SOUND

The Southeast has a rich musical history. It is home to several different musical styles.

Music in the Southeast

Bluegrass is a type of folk music played on fiddles, banjos, and guitars. It traces its roots to the Irish and Scots who settled in the Appalachian Mountains.

Blues is a style of music that was developed by W.C. Handy and other African Americans in Louisiana and Mississippi. Today, blues music is popular around the world.

Jazz music is based on African and European music styles. Jazz began in New Orleans, where a Jazz Festival is still held every year. Louis Armstrong was a famous jazz trumpet player from New Orleans.

The Cajuns of southern Louisiana have a special style of music that uses the fiddle. Zydeco, a musical style that uses the accordion, came from the same area.

Did you know that rock and roll music also started in the South? It combined country, jazz, and African American rhythms. In 1954 a young man from Memphis, Tennessee, made his first record. You may have heard of him— Elvis Presley! He became a well-known entertainer and helped make rock and roll famous.

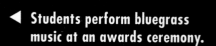

◄ Students perform bluegrass music at an awards ceremony.

Elvis Presley was a famous rock and roll artist. ▶

Soul Music

Soul music is based on African American church songs combined with blues. Aretha Franklin, who was born in Memphis, Tennessee, is known as "The Queen of Soul" because of her popular songs.

QUICK CHECK

Summarize What musical styles developed in the Southeast?

▲ Jazz musician Louis Armstrong was famous for playing his trumpet.

Check Understanding

1. **VOCABULARY** Write a sentence using these vocabulary words.

   dialect   **segregation**

2. **READING SKILL Summarize**
   Use the chart from page 182 to write about what one group of newcomers added to the culture of the Southeast.

	Summary	

3. **Write About It** Write a paragraph about how different ethnic groups can affect a region's culture.

189

Unit 4 Review and Assess

Vocabulary

Copy the sentences below on a separate sheet of paper. Use the list of vocabulary words to fill in the blanks.

wetland   renewable resource

levee   nonrenewable resource

1. A ___ is a wall built to prevent floods.

2. Petroleum is a ___.

3. A swamp is an example of a ___.

4. Trees are a ___.

Comprehension and Critical Thinking

5. Describe the climate of the Southeast.

6. **Reading Skill** What are the three types of islands found in the Southeast? Summarize.

7. **Critical Thinking** What makes the Southeast an excellent region for agriculture?

8. **Critical Thinking** How are petroleum and coal alike?

Skill

Read Circle Graphs

Write a complete sentence to answer each question.

9. How many different sources of electricity does the circle graph show?

10. Which source provides the most electricity in the United States?

Sources of Electricity in the United States

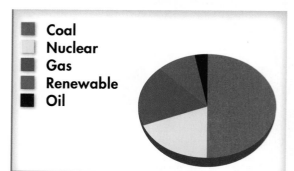

- Coal
- Nuclear
- Gas
- Renewable
- Oil

Test Preparation

Use the map and what you already know to answer the questions.

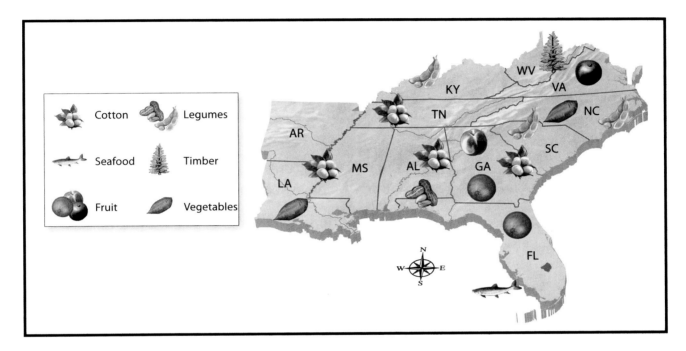

1. Which of the following states produce more than one fruit?

   A. Arkansas

   B. Georgia

   C. West Virginia

   D. Tennessee

2. Why is the Southeast a leading producer of oranges?

   A. Oranges grow well in warm climates.

   B. The orange is the official state fruit in several Southeast states.

   C. Native Americans taught settlers to grow oranges.

   D. There is a large demand for juice.

3. Which product is grown in four states in the Southeast?

   A. oranges

   B. cotton

   C. rice

   D. indigo

4. At one time, cotton and tobacco were important crops in the Southeast. Today, agriculture is more varied. Some people feel the variety is better. What is your opinion? Why?

5. Which states in the Southeast would be more likely to have fishing as an industry?

How do people affect the environment?

Write About the Big Idea

Narrative Essay
In Unit 4, you read about the geography, economy, and people of the Southeast. Review the notes in the completed foldable.

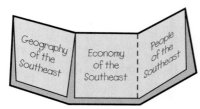

Begin your essay with an introductory paragraph describing the environment in the Southeast.

Write a paragraph describing how the geography, economy, and people of the Southeast affect the environment. The final paragraph should summarize the main ideas of the essay.

Give a News Report

Work with a partner to give a report about the issue you have researched, as if you were an anchorperson interviewing an environmentalist on a TV news show. Here's how to do your presentation:

1. Research an environmental issue such as coal mining or overfishing, that may affect the Southeast region.

2. Choose an issue to present.

3. Write a presentation. Come up with questions to discuss during the interview. Give the questions to your partner so he or she can prepare answers.

4. Draw illustrations or graphs to use as examples of the problem.

5. Present your interview to the class. Be sure to explain why the issue is important and what people are trying to do about it.

Unit 5

EXPLORE
The Big Idea

Essential Question
How do natural resources affect a region's growth?

FOLDABLES
Study Organizer

Draw Conclusions
Make a trifold book foldable to take notes as you read Unit 5. Label the three tabs **Geography**, **Economy**, and **People**.

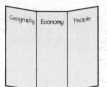

| Geography | Economy | People |

LOG ON
For more about Unit 5 go to
www.macmillanmh.com

The Midwest

PEOPLE, PLACES, AND EVENTS

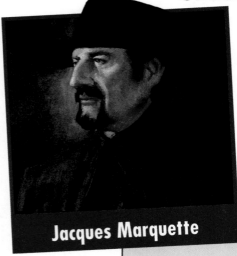

Jacques Marquette

New France

French explorers **Jacques Marquette** and Louis Jolliet explored the area of the Mississippi River in 1673. They called the area **New France**.

Today you can learn more about the Mississippi River and its explorers at the National Mississippi River Museum and Aquarium in Dubuque, Iowa..

Laura Ingalls Wilder

Wilder's Log Cabin

If you ever read a book called *Little House on the Prairie,* you read about **Laura Ingalls Wilder's** life on the frontier.

Today you can visit **Wilder's Log Cabin** in Pepin, Wisconsin.

LOG ON For more about People, Places, and Events, visit: www.macmillanmh.com

Lincoln Home National Historic Site

Abraham Lincoln

Our sixteenth President, **Abraham Lincoln**, was born and raised in Springfield, Illinois. Lincoln's parents were among the first settlers to move to the Midwest.

Today you can visit the **Lincoln Home National Historic Site** to learn more about Abraham Lincoln.

The Great Lakes

Bill Hartwig

The Great Lakes are five gigantic lakes in the Midwest. **Bill Hartwig** of the National Wildlife Refuge System is one of the many people who work to keep the Great Lakes clean.

Today the Great Lakes are the largest group of freshwater lakes in the world. They're so big you can see them from space!

Midwest Region

Midwest

The Midwest is home to both important and fun places to visit.

1 Mount Rushmore honors Presidents Washington, Jefferson, T. Roosevelt, and Lincoln. Each head is about 60 feet tall.

kawea

ND
Bismarck ★

SD
Lake Oahe

0   100   200 kilometers

1 BLACK HILLS   Pierre ★

BADLANDS

N
W E
S

NE

KS

Arkansas River

5 The American Bison was very important to Native Americans. Today there are about 350,000 in the United States.

2 Cheese and other dairy products are a very important part of the economy of the Midwest.

3 Some say that the giant footsteps of Paul Bunyan and his blue ox, Babe, created Minnesota's 10,000 lakes.

5

3

MESABI RANGE

Tettegouche State Park

Lake Superior

Keweenaw Peninsula

Apostle Islands National Lakeshore

UPPER PENINSULA

MN

SUPERIOR UPLAND

St. Paul ★

Mississippi River

Lake Huron

Lake Ontario

WI **2**

LOWER PENINSULA

Lake Michigan

MI

Madison ★

Lansing ★

Detroit •

Lake Erie

IA

CENTRAL PLAINS

Chicago •

ALLEGHENY PLATEAU

G R E A T   P L A I N S

Platte River

Missouri River

Des Moines ★

Wabash River

OH

Lincoln ★

IN **4**

Indianapolis ★

Columbus ★

MO

IL

Springfield ★

Wayne National Forest

Ohio River

Topeka ★

St. Louis •

Jefferson City ★

Ohio River

4 The Indianapolis 500 is one of the most famous car races in the world.

INTERIOR PLAINS

OZARK PLATEAU

Mark Twain National Forest

ethanol 17

Lesson 1

VOCABULARY

fertile p. 200

prairie p. 202

READING SKILL

Draw Conclusions

Copy the chart. Use it to draw conclusions about the Mississippi River.

Text Clues	Conclusion

STANDARDS FOCUS

SOCIAL STUDIES — People, Places, and Environments

GEOGRAPHY — Physical Systems

The Geography of the Midwest

Visual Preview

How have the Great Lakes affected the Midwest?

A The Great Lakes make a good home for plants and animals.

B The Midwest has many rivers that help make the soil fertile for farming.

C The Midwest has plains, hills, mountains, and badlands.

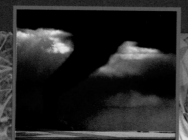

D The Midwest has hot summers, cold winters, and seasonal storms.

A A LAND FORMED BY WATER

The 12 states in the Midwest region are in the middle of the United States. This region is known as the Heartland of America. Many amazing plants and animals make this region unique and beautiful.

The Midwest region sits between the Appalachian Mountains and the Rocky Mountains. Although there are no oceans in the Midwest, there's plenty of water. Thousands of years ago, huge glaciers covered parts of the Midwest. As these gigantic sheets of ice moved slowly across the region, they flattened the land and carved out giant holes. When the glaciers melted, they filled the holes with water.

Today the holes created by the glaciers are called the Great Lakes. Lake Superior, Lake Michigan, Lake Huron, and Lake Erie are in the Midwest. Lake Ontario is in the Northeast. Thousands of smaller lakes were also formed by the glaciers. Minnesota, for example, has 22,000 lakes. All of these lakes make a good home for the region's plants and animals.

The plants and animals of the Midwest have adapted to different landforms. They have also adapted to hot summers and cold winters.

Plants and Animals of the Midwest

Foxglove Beard Tongue

White-tailed Jackrabbit

Prairie Cone Flower

Burrowing Owl

Black-eyed Susan

Red-tailed Hawk

QUICK CHECK

Draw Conclusions **Where did the water in the Great Lakes first come from?**

199

B FLOWING RIVERS

When the glaciers melted thousands of years ago, they created rivers. These rivers carried soil from the north and brought it south. The soil was **fertile**, or filled with vitamins and minerals that plants need to grow. Many of the states in the Midwest, such as Iowa and Ohio, now have lots of fertile soil. Fertile soil lets farmers produce crops that are healthy.

Several big rivers run through the region. More than half of the Mississippi River is in the Midwest. The Ohio River creates a southern border for Ohio, Indiana, and Illinois. The Missouri River flows into the Mississippi from the west.

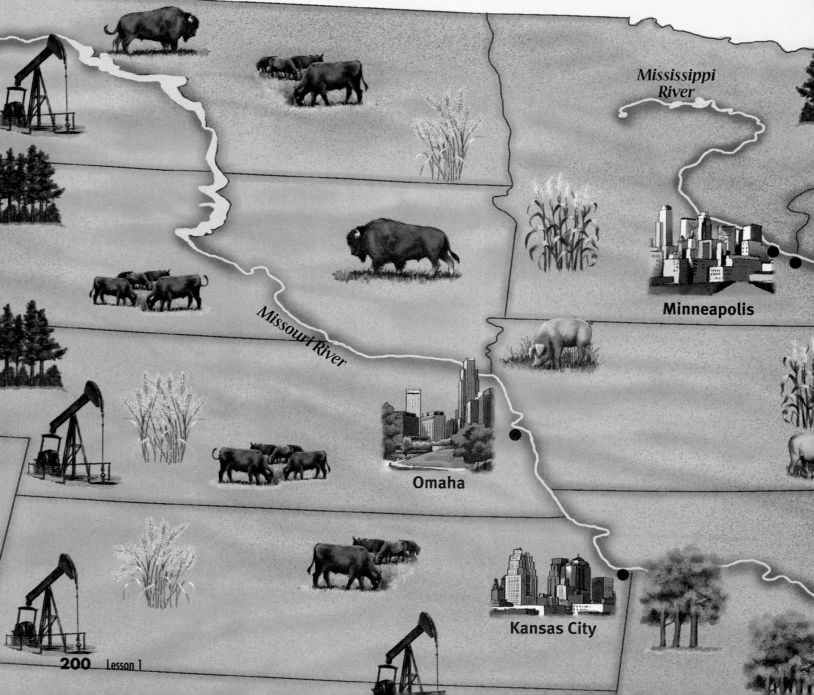

Mississippi River

Minneapolis

Missouri River

Omaha

Kansas City

Samuel Clemens, also known as Mark Twain, became one of our country's best-known writers. Many of Twain's novels take place on or near the Mississippi River.

Samuel Clemens

The Missouri is more than 2,300 miles long. This river has been nicknamed the "Big Muddy" for the amount of dirt it carries in its waters. To get an idea of how much water is in the Midwest, take a look at the map below. You can see that many of the region's cities were built along river banks.

QUICK CHECK

Summarize How did glaciers improve Midwestern soil?

St. Paul

Cincinnati

Ohio River

Louisville

St. Louis

201

C LANDFORMS OF THE MIDWEST

The Midwest is mostly flat land. There are very few hills or mountains. When glaciers moved down the region, they flattened hills and filled valleys with dirt. This created plains, or flat lands covered by grasses and wildflowers. Plains covered by grasses and wildflowers are called **prairies**.

Mountains and Hills

Glaciers didn't flatten all of the hills and mountains in the Midwest. There are hills in parts of Ohio, Michigan, and even Illinois. The farther you move away from the Great Lakes, the higher the land gets. The plains slowly give way to hills, and by the time you get as far away from the Great Lakes as you can within the region, you are in the mountains.

Harney Peak, in the Black Hills mountains of South Dakota, is 7,242 feet above sea level. Underneath the Black Hills is Wind Cave. Wind Cave has more than 100 miles of winding passages. Alvin McDonald explored the cave in the 1890s. Read about his experience below.

Primary Sources

They are still finding new rooms at the Wind Cave and we have about come to the conclusion there is no end to it.

Alvin McDonald

Write About It What did Alvin McDonald conclude about Wind Cave?

The Badlands

The Midwest has lakes, rivers, prairies, and mountains with caves. Is that all, you ask? No! There are also badlands in the Midwest. Badlands are very dry lands that have been chipped away by wind and water. The wind and water carved out canyons, ravines, gullies (narrow and deep holes that were created by water), and other such landforms. Badlands usually have a spectacular color that ranges from dark black or blue to bright red.

It just so happens that all of the badlands in the United States are in the Midwest. In North Dakota, there's Theodore Roosevelt National Park, while Badlands National Park is in South Dakota. There's also Toadstool Geologic

PLACES

Wind Cave National Park is home to one of the world's longest caves and 28,295 acres of prairie, pine forest, and diverse wildlife.

Wind Cave

Park in the Oglala National Grassland of Nebraska. Wind, water, and erosion have twisted the peaks and rocks of these badlands into unusual shapes.

QUICK CHECK

Summarize Describe the landforms of the Midwest region.

Badlands National Park, South Dakota

Tornadoes whirl around at speeds of up to 200 miles per hour.

Temperatures in the Midwest can vary widely. The areas around the Great Lakes may also experience what is called the lake effect. Since water takes longer to heat and cool than land, the air over the water is often hotter or cooler than the air over the land. When winds blow across the lakes, they carry this hot or cool air over the land, affecting the temperature.

Storms occur in the Midwest, too. In winter, heavy snowstorms whip across the plains. In summer, strong winds can form dangerous, destructive tornadoes.

QUICK CHECK

Cause and Effect How do the Great Lakes cause climate changes in the Midwest?

Check Understanding

1. **VOCABULARY** Summarize this lesson in a paragraph using the vocabulary words below.

   fertile   **prairie**

2. **READING SKILL** Draw Conclusions Use the chart from page 198 to write a paragraph about why the Mississippi River is so large.

Text Clues	Conclusion

3. **Write About It** Write a paragraph about how the geography of the Midwest drew people to settle there.

EXPLORE
The
Big
Idea

Chart and Graph Skills

Compare Bar and Line Graphs

VOCABULARY
bar graph
line graph

A graph is a special kind of diagram that shows facts clearly. A **bar graph** uses bars to show information. A **line graph** shows how something has changed over time.

The bar graph below shows the value of Iowa's top five farm products in 2004. The line graph below shows how the population of the Midwest has changed.

Learn It

- Graph A is a bar graph. It shows the value of Iowa's top farm products in 2004. The height of the bars tells the value of each product in 2004.

- Graph B is a line graph. The numbers on the left of the line graph represent the population of the Midwest region. The labels at the bottom show the years that the graph covers.

Try It

- What was the population of the Midwest in 1910?

- What product had the most value in Iowa in 2004?

Apply It

- Find the number and kinds of pets your classmates have. Decide which kind of graph would be best to show the information. Make the graph.

A: Iowa's Top Farm Products, 2004

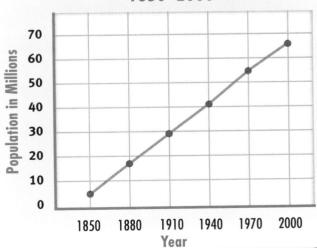
B: Population of the Midwest, 1850–2000

Lesson 2

The Economy of the Midwest

VOCABULARY

iron p. 208

ore p. 208

open-pit mining p. 208

agribusiness p. 210

mass production p. 212

assembly line p. 212

READING SKILL

Draw Conclusions
Copy the chart. Use it to draw conclusions about the future of the Midwest's economy.

Text Clues	Conclusion

STANDARDS FOCUS

| SOCIAL STUDIES | Production, Distribution, and Consumption |
| GEOGRAPHY | Environment and Society |

Cleveland Cliffs Iron Ore Mine and Mill in Republic, Michigan

Visual Preview

How have people made a living in the Midwest over time?

A Natural resources have always been an important part of the region's economy.

B By the 1900s, the Midwest had become a giant in steel production.

C Manufacturing and agriculture are important to the Midwest economy.

D Today the service and technology industries are important to the Midwest.

206

A A RICH LAND

The Midwest's economy starts with the land. The land provides energy sources, such as coal, oil, and natural gas, as well as metals, such as iron and copper.

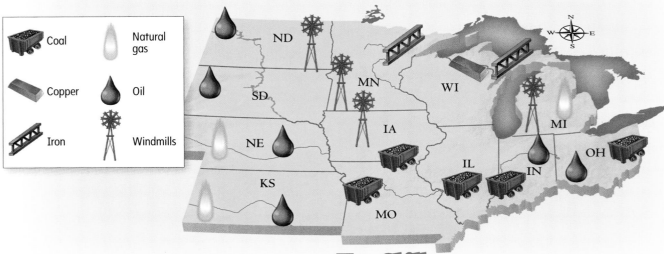

Resources of the Midwest

Coal	Natural gas		
Copper	Oil		
Iron	Windmills		

Map Skill

LOCATION **Which states have both oil and coal as a natural resource?**

You already know that a region's economy depends heavily on the natural resources found in the region. The Midwest has many.

The region's water resources include the Great Lakes and rivers such as the Ohio, Mississippi, and Missouri. These waterways are used to ship goods across the country.

The rich soil of the Midwest provides ideal conditions for farming. When you go underground or in hills and mountains you find metals. Metals are a valuable resource.

That's not all the Midwest has. It also has wind! Strong winds that blow across the Midwest are an incredible energy source. They turn the blades of wind turbines that are used to create electricity.

QUICK CHECK

Summarize **What energy resources can be found in the Midwest?**

B MINING FOR METAL

Iron is an important resource in the Midwest. Iron is valuable because it can be turned into steel—a strong metal used to make buildings, tools, and cars. In the 1800s, iron **ore** was found in Minnesota and Michigan. Ore is a rock with iron or another mineral inside. Iron mining became big business in the Midwest.

Minnesota has one of the richest supplies of iron ore in the world. The iron ore is found just below the surface of the ground so miners don't need to dig deep tunnels to reach it. Instead, miners dig a pit, remove the top layer of earth, and scoop up the ore beneath. This is called **open-pit mining**.

Steel and Skyscrapers

Steel changed the economy of the Midwest. The demand for steel across the United States soared in the 1800s and 1900s. Factories sprang up to turn the region's iron into steel.

Open-Pit Mine

surface

access road

pit bottom

ore

Open-pit iron ore mine in Republic, Michigan

By 1900 the Midwest had become a giant in steel production. Steel was used to make railroad cars, bridges, tall buildings, planes, and cars.

Sears Tower

QUICK CHECK

Main Idea and Details **How did steel change the economy of the Midwest?**

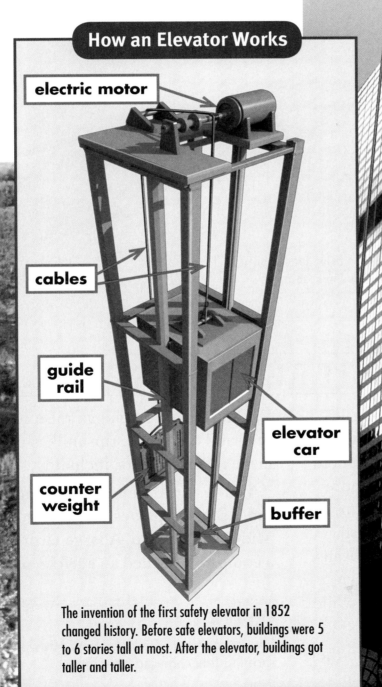

How an Elevator Works

electric motor

cables

guide rail

elevator car

counter weight

buffer

The invention of the first safety elevator in 1852 changed history. Before safe elevators, buildings were 5 to 6 stories tall at most. After the elevator, buildings got taller and taller.

Soybeans being loaded onto a truck in Minnesota

C AGRICULTURE ON THE PRAIRIE

Early Midwestern farms were small. A farm family ate most of what they produced. After machines were invented to help farmers plant and harvest more crops faster, farmers could raise crops for money. The most important cash crops in the Midwest are corn, soybeans, and wheat. Iowa grows the most corn and soybeans in the United States, while Kansas raises the most wheat.

Dairy farming is also important to the Midwestern economy. Many farms in Wisconsin and Michigan raise cows for their milk. Some of this milk is used to make milk products, including cheese.

Midwestern farming has changed over time. Big companies now own some Midwest farmland. A large farm owned by a company is called an **agribusiness**.

QUICK CHECK

Sequence Events **Describe how Midwestern farming has changed over time.**

Global Connections

Kansas Wheat

Midwestern crops are used to feed people and animals across the United States. This is how the region earned its nickname "America's Breadbasket." These crops are also used to feed people around the world.

The Midwest does a huge business in farm exports, or the sale of crops to other nations. In 2003, Kansas farms earned $3 billion by selling their goods to other countries. The most important Kansas crop is wheat. More than half of Kansas's wheat is sold to other countries.

Japan, Mexico, Djibouti, and Nigeria are some of the countries that buy Kansas wheat. Japan is a nation with little land and many people. This means it must buy agricultural products from other countries. Although Mexico and Nigeria are nations with plenty of farmland, wheat does not grow well in their countries' hot climates.

Djibouti

▲ Workers in Djibouti load bags of wheat from the United States onto a ship headed for Ethiopia.

A wheat field in Kansas

Kansas

Write About It Write a paragraph about why other countries may import agricultural products from the United States.

Assembly Line

Ⓓ CHANGING THE WORLD

In the early 1900s, many Midwestern cities became manufacturing centers. Detroit, Michigan, was famous for cars, Toledo, Ohio, for glass, and Minneapolis, Minnesota, for flour mills. As machines did more and more of the work on farms, people who lived in the countryside moved to Midwestern cities to find jobs in factories.

New Methods of Manufacturing

In Detroit, carmaker Henry Ford spent years researching ways to build cars quickly and cheaply. In 1913 Ford began creating cars through **mass production**. This is the manufacturing of many products at one time. Ford made thousands of cars on an **assembly line**,

or a line of workers and machines that put together a product in steps. Each worker or machine does one task, again and again. The diagram above shows the steps from start to finish in Ford's early assembly line.

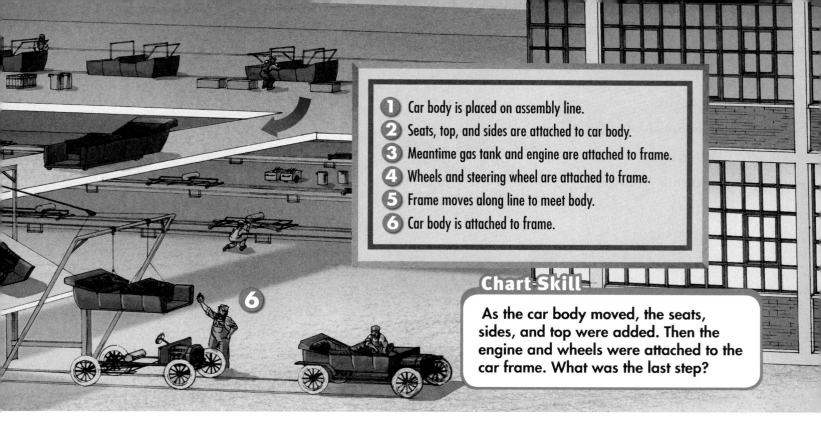

1. Car body is placed on assembly line.
2. Seats, top, and sides are attached to car body.
3. Meantime gas tank and engine are attached to frame.
4. Wheels and steering wheel are attached to frame.
5. Frame moves along line to meet body.
6. Car body is attached to frame.

Chart Skill

As the car body moved, the seats, sides, and top were added. Then the engine and wheels were attached to the car frame. What was the last step?

Working in the Midwest Today

Jobs in the Midwest have continued to change. More people work in the service industry. Some service workers have jobs in hotels, banks, or insurance companies.

Many Midwesterners have jobs in technology. Illinois has one of the world's largest laboratories for studying atoms—Fermilab. Missouri is a leader in medical research, or looking for ways to cure diseases. Slowly, new industries will replace the factories that once led the Midwestern economy.

QUICK CHECK

Main Idea and Details How did Henry Ford change the car industry?

◀ Fermilab in Illinois

Check Understanding

1. **VOCABULARY** Write a sentence for each vocabulary word.

   iron   agribusiness   mass production

2. **READING SKILL** Draw Conclusions Use the chart from page 206 to write about why the Midwest is a good place for both agriculture and industry.

Text Clues	Conclusion

 EXPLORE The Big Idea

3. **Write About It** Write a paragraph about iron ore in the Midwest.

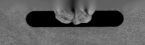

Lesson 3

VOCABULARY

descendants p. 215

pioneer p. 217

migration p. 217

tradition p. 219

READING SKILL

Draw Conclusions

Copy the chart. As you read, list reasons why people came to the Midwest.

Text Clues	Conclusion

STANDARDS FOCUS

SOCIAL STUDIES Culture

GEOGRAPHY Human Systems

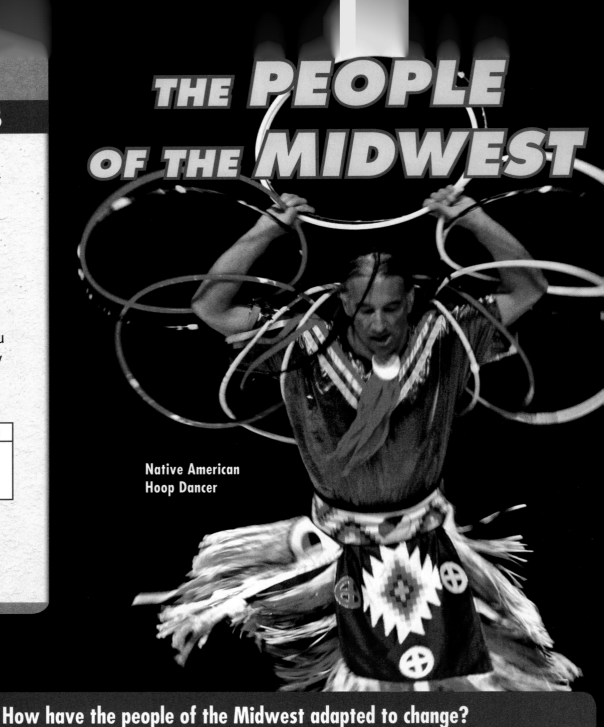

THE PEOPLE OF THE MIDWEST

Native American
Hoop Dancer

Visual Preview

How have the people of the Midwest adapted to change?

A Native Americans were the first Midwesterners. Many of their mounds remain.

B Many people from Europe made the Midwest their home.

C Today immigrants to the Midwest come from all around the world.

D The Midwest is home to many great artists, musicians, writers, and athletes.

A THE FIRST MIDWESTERNERS

Native Americans were the first people of the Midwest. Today Midwesterners are the descendants, or the children and grandchildren, of Native Americans and immigrants who have come to the Midwest from around the world.

Hundreds of years ago, a group of people that were called mound builders lived in the Midwest. They were called mound builders because they built large hills. Mound builders farmed, traded, and built cities. At one time, one of the largest Mississippian cities, Cahokia, may have had up to 20,000 people living there. The mound cultures disappeared sometime around 1300. They were replaced by other cultures.

One of these cultures is the Ojibwa (sometimes called Chippewa). They lived in present-day Michigan and Ohio. The Ojibwa are part of a group of Native Americans called the Eastern Woodlands peoples. They hunted, fished, and sometimes farmed in the forests and waters of the Midwest before Europeans came to North America. Today there are many Ojibwa reservations in Wisconsin, Michigan, and Minnesota.

The Lakota live in the Midwest, too. They are part of a group known as the Plains peoples. In the past, they lived on the plains of Nebraska, North Dakota, South Dakota, and Minnesota. The Lakota depended on buffalo for food, clothing, and shelter. Today Lakota communities in the Midwest mix modern culture with traditional ways of life.

QUICK CHECK

Summarize **What groups of people lived in the Midwest hundreds of years ago?**

Grave Creek Burial Mound ▶

Early settlers to the Midwest traveled by flatboat.

ⓑ PEOPLE OF THE MIDWEST

In the 1500s, European fur traders began exploring the Midwest for a new and inexpensive supply of furs. Around 1770, a fur trader named Jean Baptiste Pointe du Sable began a trading post near Lake Michigan. Du Sable was from the French colony of Haiti, an island in the Caribbean Sea. Du Sable's trading post grew into the city of Chicago.

Heading West

Fur traders shipped their goods to Europe from ports in the Northeast.

Many people in these eastern cities learned about the fertile Midwestern soil. Fertile soil meant a chance for them to make a good living as a farmer. Many decided to move to the Midwest in search of this rich land with endless possibilities.

As more people traveled west, new trails opened. Later settlers traveled along these new trails in covered wagons. These wagons were pulled by horses, mules, or oxen. By 1850, more than five million people had settled in the Midwest.

Most of the Native Americans' land in Ohio, Indiana, and Illinois was taken by soldiers for the new settlers.

These first settlers to travel west were known as **pioneers**. The parents of Abraham Lincoln, our nation's sixteenth president, were pioneers.

New Immigrants

In the late 1800s and early 1900s, the population of the Midwest became more diverse. Norwegian farmers moved to Minnesota and people from Czechoslovakia worked the land in Nebraska. Polish immigrants found factory jobs in Illinois and thousands of Germans and Italians settled in Wisconsin, Missouri, and Ohio.

EVENT

Thousands of African Americans traveled on the **Underground Railroad** to escape slavery in the South. By 1850 nearly 100,000 African Americans had fled to the Midwest and Canada.

Underground Railroad

African Americans in the Midwest

African Americans headed to the Midwest from the South to escape slavery. They traveled on what is now known as the Underground Railroad—a network of people who helped enslaved people escape. William Wells Brown escaped slavery in 1833:

"As we traveled towards a land of liberty, my heart would at times leap for joy."

Later, African Americans moved from the South to the Midwest to find jobs and equality. Most settled in factory cities in Illinois, Ohio, and Michigan. Their move north between the years of 1914 and 1950 is called the Great **Migration**. A migration is a journey from one place to another.

QUICK CHECK

Summarize **Describe the different people that have come to the Midwest.**

◀ Midwesterners today come from around the world.

C THE MIDWEST TODAY

People from across the world continue to move to the Midwest. Many Mexicans have settled in Chicago. Immigrants from East Africa and Southeast Asia live in St. Paul and Minneapolis. Detroit has the largest population of Arab Americans in the United States. Today modern immigrants arrive by car, bus, or plane, not by flatboat or wagon.

Celebrating Cultures and Traditions

Different cultures make the Midwest fun and exciting. Many types of celebrations honor the region's ethnic heritage. People in Holland, Michigan, celebrate their Dutch roots with a tulip festival each spring. Milwaukee, Wisconsin, has a large German festival every summer, and St. Louis, Missouri, holds a Japanese festival every fall.

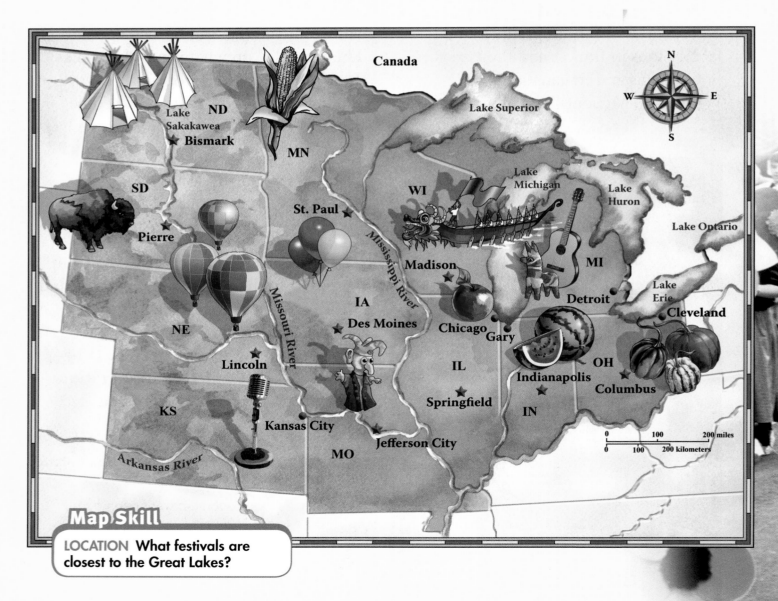

Map Skill

LOCATION **What festivals are closest to the Great Lakes?**

Midwesterners also honor their region's history, weather, and **traditions**, or customs, that make the region a great place to live. St. Paul, Minnesota, holds a Winter Carnival to celebrate the region's cold weather. The Corn Palace in South Dakota is decorated with thousands of cornstalks to celebrate farming. St. Louis is proud of its history as the "Gateway to the West."

Dutch descendants celebrate their heritage during the Tulip Festival in Holland, Michigan. ▼

Legend

🚣	Great Mideast Dragon Boat Festival in Racine, WI
🍎	Apple Festival in Long Grove, IL
🍉	Brownstown Melonfest in Brownstown, IN
🎃	Circleville Pumpkin Show in Circleville, OH
🤹	PuppetFest Midwest in Trenton, MO
🎈	Iowa State Fair in Des Moines, IA
🎸	Tulipanes Latino Art & Film Festival in Holland, MI
🎺	Kansas City Kansas Street Blues Festival
🎈	Hot Air Balloon Festival in Wakefield, NE
🦬	Buffalo Roundup and Arts Festival in Custer State Park, SD
	National boundary
	State boundary
●	Major city
★	State capital
🛖	Northern Plains Indian Culture Fest Stanton, ND
🌽	Hinckley Corn & Clover Festival in Hinckly, MN

Three friends learned that pollution was threatening the brook trout in streams near their township. In an effort to protect the fish, the girls formed a group called Save Our Streams (SOS). They wrote letters and talked with people and leaders in the area to work on a plan for keeping the streams clean.

Write About It Write a letter to your local newspaper expressing your opinion about an issue.

MIDWEST ART, MUSIC, AND FUN

Throughout history, the states of the Midwest have been home to many great artists, musicians, writers, and athletes. Some of our nation's best-known writers, for example, are from the Midwest. Laura Ingalls Wilder wrote amazing stories about her life as a pioneer. The poet Thomas Stearns Eliot, known as T. S. Eliot, was born in St. Louis. Read what he had to say about it.

The Midwest is also known for its music. What kinds of music do you like? In the Midwest, the best answer is all of them! Cleveland disc jockey Alan Freed helped develop rock and roll in the 1950s. Today, Cleveland is home to the Rock and Roll Hall of Fame. Detroit is famous for soul music. Kansas City is known for jazz. Bluegrass star Alison Krauss grew up in Illinois.

> I am very well satisfied with having been born in St. Louis.
>
> —T.S. ELIOT

Sculptor Korczak Ziolkowski moved to South Dakota in 1947 to carve the Crazy Horse monument out of the Black Hills mountains. Although he died in 1982, his children continue working on the monument.

The 500 Mile Race

The largest sport facility in the world is in Indianapolis, Indiana, and is called the Indianapolis Motor Speedway. Every year, it holds the Indy 500 race over Memorial weekend. In 2006, the Indy 500 race celebrated its 90th anniversary. But that's not all that happens at the Speedway. Famous races such as the Allstate 400 and the United States Grand Prix are also held there. These races attract thousands of visitors from around the world.

▲ The Indianapolis 500 is held every year in Indianapolis, Indiana.

QUICK CHECK

Summarize What are some of the things people in the Midwest do for fun?

George Clinton and Parliament-Funkadelic perform at the Rock and Roll Hall of Fame. ▼

Check Understanding

1. **VOCABULARY** Use each vocabulary word to describe the people of the Midwest.

   pioneer **migration** **tradition**

2. **READING SKILL** Draw Conclusions Use the chart from page 214 to write about why you think the Midwest inspires so many writers and artists.

Text Clues	Conclusion

3. **Write About It** Write a short essay about what the Great Migration might have been like for the people who migrated.

Vocabulary

Copy the sentences below. Use the list of vocabulary words to fill in the blanks.

mass production	iron
fertile	pioneer

1. Wheat and corn are grown in the _____ soil of the Midwest.

2. Henry Ford was one of the first to use _____ in manufacturing.

3. Steel is made in part from a metal known as _____.

4. An early settler of the Midwest is called a _____.

Comprehension and Critical Thinking

5. How were the Great Lakes formed?

6. Who was Jean Baptiste Pointe du Sable?

7. **Reading Skill** Why is the Midwest home to so many musical styles? Draw conclusions.

8. **Critical Thinking** What do you think it was like to be a pioneer?

Skill

Use Line and Bar Graphs

Write a complete sentence to answer each question.

9. Which state has the largest population?

10. Which state has the smallest population?

Population of Great Lakes States, 2005

Bar graph with y-axis "People in Millions" ranging 0 to 14, x-axis "States": Ohio, Michigan, Indiana, Illinois, Wisconsin, Minnesota.

Test Preparation

Read the paragraphs. Then answer the questions.

Without warm ocean breezes, much of the Midwest is extremely cold in the winter. Icy winds travel across the plains, chilling everything in their path. Blizzards, or winter storms with strong winds and snow, can form and become dangerous.

Cities near the Great Lakes receive the heaviest snowfall. This lake effect snow occurs when cold, dry air from Canada meets warmer, damp air over the Great Lakes. Moisture in the air cools and becomes snow. Some areas can receive more than 200 inches of lake effect snow each year.

1. What conclusions can you draw about winters in the Midwest?

   A. It is warmer inland in winter.

   B. Most people leave the Midwest during the winter.

   C. The weather in Canada affects winters in the Midwest.

   D. The weather in Canada is cold.

2. What causes lake effect snow?

   A. temperatures fall below freezing

   B. dry air from Canada meets damp air over the Great Lakes

   C. winds travel across the plains

   D. cold air comes from Canada

3. What cities receive the heaviest snowfall?

   A. Most of the cities in the Midwest receive heavy snowfall.

   B. Cities near the Great Lakes

   C. Cities in Canada

   D. None of the cities in the Midwest experience heavy snowfall.

4. How do you think the lake effect snow affects the people of the Midwest?

5. What might it be like to live in a part of the Midwest that has an extreme climate, such as the Badlands or a desert?

The Big Idea Activities

How do natural resources affect a region's growth?

Write About the Big Idea

Expository Essay
Use the Unit 5 foldable to help you write an essay that answers the Big Idea question, "How do natural resources affect a region's growth?" Be sure to begin your essay with an introduction. Use the notes you wrote under each tab in the foldable for details to support each main idea. End with a concluding paragraph that answers the question.

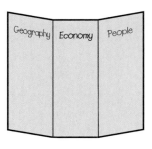

Create a Diorama

Work in a small group to create a diorama showing a pioneer family coming to the Midwest on a flatboat or covered wagon. Here's how you can get started:

1. Research the pioneers who headed west.

2. Choose the structures you would like to represent in your diorama.

3. Choose the materials you will use to build your diorama.

4. Build the pieces and assemble the diorama.

5. Write a paragraph telling what is happening in your diorama.

Unit 6

EXPLORE
The
Big
Idea

Essential Question
How do people adapt to their environments?

FOLDABLES
Study Organizer

Cause and Effect
Use a layered book foldable to take notes as you read Unit 6. Write **The Southwest** across the bottom of the foldable. Label the layers **Geography**, **Economy**, and **People**. Use the foldable to organize information as you read.

People
Economy
Geography
The Southwest

LOG
ON

For more about Unit 6 go to
www.macmillanmh.com

The Southwest

225

PEOPLE, PLACES, AND EVENTS

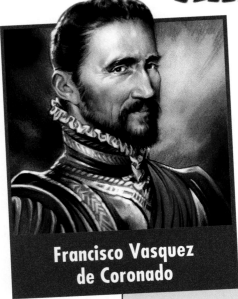

Francisco Vasquez de Coronado

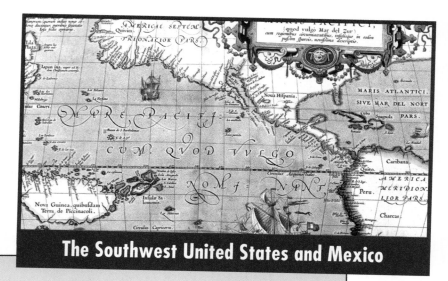

The Southwest United States and Mexico

Between 1540 and 1542, a Spanish explorer named **Francisco Vasquez de Coronado** led a group of people in a search for cities of gold. Although he did not find any gold, Coronado explored **the Southwest United States and Mexico.**

Today you can visit the Coronado National Memorial in Arizona.

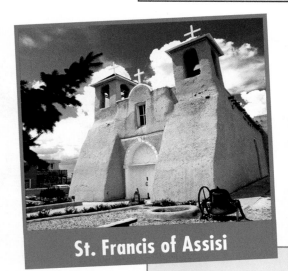

St. Francis of Assisi

Traditional Mexican Dancers

Before the Southwest became part of the United States, most of it belonged to Mexico. Mexican culture can be seen in buildings such as the **St. Francis of Assisi** church.

Today you can watch **traditional Mexican dancers** at festivals throughout the region.

LOG ON

For more about People, Places, and Events, visit:
www.macmillanmh.com

National Cowboys of Color Museum and Hall of Fame

Nat Love

By the mid-1800s, ranching and cattle herding were important to the economy of the Southwest. **Nat Love**, Addison Jones, and Bill Pickett were famous African American cowboys.

Today you can visit the **National Cowboys of Color Museum and Hall of Fame** in Fort Worth, Texas.

The Grand Canyon

John Wesley Powell

The Grand Canyon is a beautiful natural landform in our country. **John Wesley Powell** was one of the first explorers to see its deep ravines and the rushing Colorado River.

Today you can visit Grand Canyon National Park in Arizona and explore its many trails.

Southwest Region

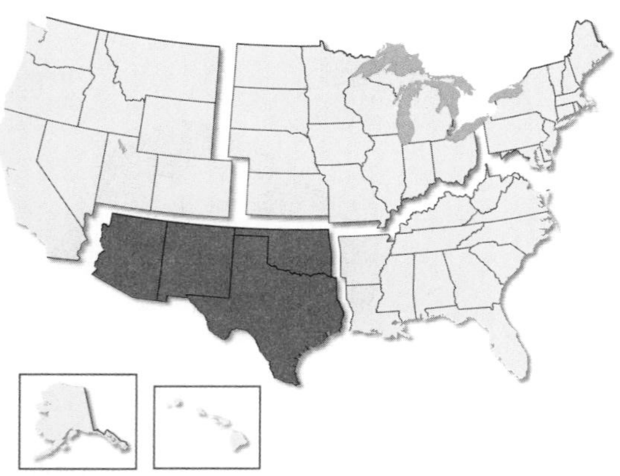

The hot, dry climate of the Southwest hosts plants, animals, and landforms.

1 Chili peppers are often used in southwestern cooking.

Lake Mead

GRA CAN

Colorado River

2

AZ

Phoenix ★

SONORAN DESERT

Gulf of California

5 The Alamo, a Spanish mission, was the site of an 1836 battle between Texas and Mexico. Today it is a museum devoted to Texas history.

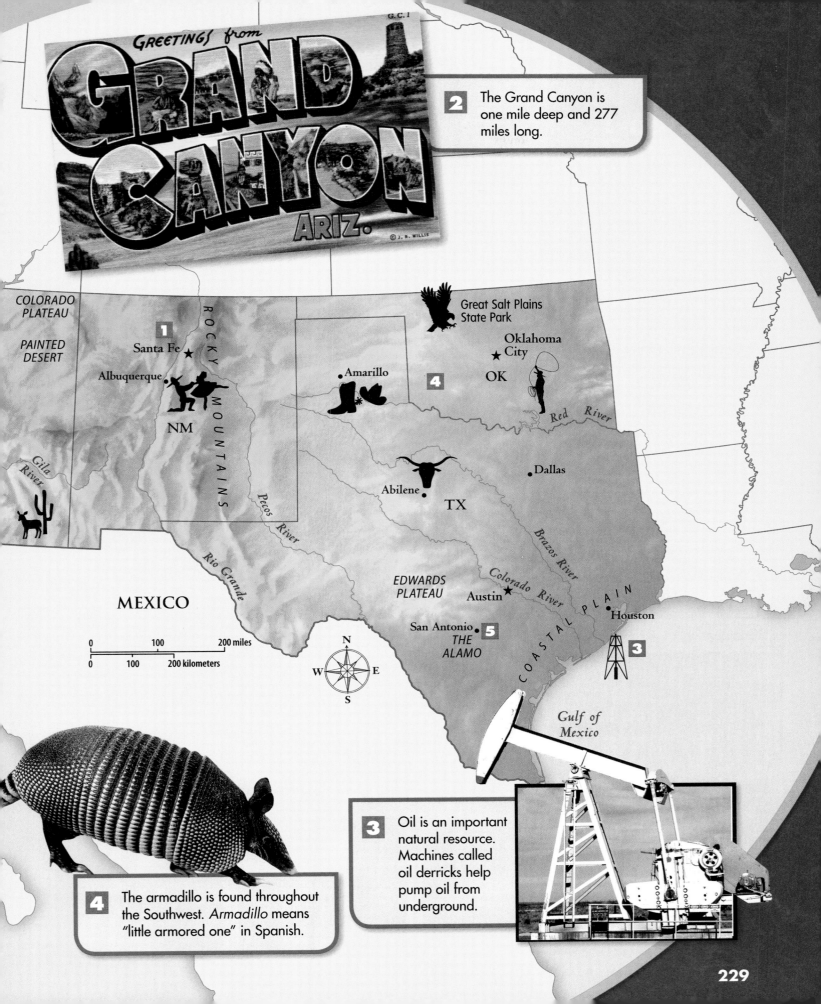

Greetings from GRAND CANYON ARIZ.

G.C. 1

© J. R. WILLIS

2 The Grand Canyon is one mile deep and 277 miles long.

COLORADO PLATEAU

PAINTED DESERT

Gila River

1

Santa Fe ★

Albuquerque •

NM

ROCKY MOUNTAINS

Pecos River

Rio Grande

MEXICO

Amarillo •

4

Great Salt Plains State Park

Oklahoma City ★

OK

Red River

Dallas •

Abilene •

TX

Brazos River

EDWARDS PLATEAU

Colorado River

Austin ★

San Antonio • **5**
THE ALAMO

Houston •

3

COASTAL PLAIN

Gulf of Mexico

0   100   200 miles
0   100   200 kilometers

N
W   E
S

3 Oil is an important natural resource. Machines called oil derricks help pump oil from underground.

4 The armadillo is found throughout the Southwest. *Armadillo* means "little armored one" in Spanish.

THE GEOGRAPHY OF THE SOUTHWEST

Lesson 1

VOCABULARY

mesa p. 233

butte p. 233

canyon p. 234

drought p. 236

aquifer p. 237

READING SKILL

Cause and Effect

Copy the chart. As you read, fill it in with information about how the geography of the Southwest formed.

Cause	→	Effect
	→	
	→	
	→	

STANDARDS FOCUS

SOCIAL STUDIES People, Places, and Environments

GEOGRAPHY Physical Systems

Visual Preview

How have the people of the Southwest adapted to their environment?

A The Southwest has coastline, plains, prairies, deserts, and mountains.

B Erosion has caused some strange landforms in the Southwest.

C The Southwest has long rivers.

D The Southwest has a dry climate with little rainfall.

Ⓐ FROM COAST TO PLAINS

There are only four states in the Southwest region, but the area it covers is huge. It's no surprise that this region has many different landforms and environments.

There's only one state in the Southwest that has a coastline—Texas. This coastline runs along the Gulf of Mexico. A gulf is a body of water that is partly surrounded by land. The flat lowland next to the coast is called the Gulf Coastal Plain.

As you move inland from the Texas coastline, the land rises. You soon come to broad, rolling plains which continue into Oklahoma. The plains are dry, but grass grows well there. This area is a vast prairie, or grassland. Once, Native American groups and European settlers hunted buffalo on these plains. Today cattle graze here instead.

Other Landforms

The Southwest isn't just coast and plains. In parts of Texas, there are swamps. There are also many deserts in the Southwest. All the Southwestern states have mountains. The plants and animals in each of these environments have adapted to their surroundings.

Plants and Animals of the Southwest

Prickly-pear Cactus

Roadrunner

Joshua Tree

Kangaroo Rat

Saguaro Cactus

Jackrabbit

QUICK CHECK

Cause and Effect **How has the use of the prairie in the Southwest changed?**

STRANGE LANDFORMS

Picture a tower of rock 1,000 feet tall that looks like a ship. Another rock has a hole through it. Still others look like mittens sticking out of the ground. Why are the rocks such unusual shapes?

Eroded Rock

The strange forms were made by erosion. Over millions of years, wind wore away the softer rock, leaving the remaining harder rock in unusual shapes. Some of the strangest formations are in an area of Arizona and Utah called Monument Valley.

Plateaus, Mesas, and Buttes

Look at the map on pages 228 and 229. Find the place where Utah, Colorado, Arizona, and New Mexico meet. Do you see why this spot is known as the Four Corners? This is where you find a huge area called the Colorado Plateau that extends into four states. A plateau is an area that rises steeply from the land

butte

In Monument Valley, Arizona, the softer rocks have worn away. The harder rocks that remain look like giant mittens.

around it. At 130,000 square miles, the Colorado Plateau is larger than the entire state of New Mexico!

Erosion has created other unusual landforms, too. Land that looks like high hills with flat tops are called **mesas** from the Spanish word for table. The region also has **buttes**. A butte is a hill with a flat top and its width is smaller than the width of a mesa.

PLACES

One special place on the Colorado Plateau is **the Painted Desert** in Arizona. Here the sides of the mesas and buttes look like an artist has used a giant brush to paint stripes of blue, purple, orange, red, pink, and gold.

The Painted Desert

QUICK CHECK

Summarize **What caused the strange rock formations seen in the Southwest?**

plateau

C · RIVERS

According to a famous legend, a giant named Paul Bunyan dragged his pick behind him as he walked across Arizona. The pick left a gash in the ground a mile deep and almost 300 miles long!

Today we call this area the Grand Canyon. A **canyon** is a deep valley with steep rocky walls. Of course, we know the Grand Canyon was really formed by the Colorado River.

The Colorado River starts in the Rocky Mountains. From there, it flows through five states and empties into the Gulf of Mexico. On its way, the river carries along dirt and pebbles. As the dirt and pebbles flow downriver, they rub against the river banks. Over millions of years, the dirt and pebbles carried in the running water wore away softer rocks and carved out the Grand Canyon.

The Grand Canyon is deeper than 22 football fields are long.

How grand is the Grand Canyon? At places it is a mile deep. If there was a bridge across the Grand Canyon at its widest point (18 miles), it would take you about six hours to walk across it. Read what President Roosevelt said about the Grand Canyon.

> The Grand Canyon fills me with awe. . . . [It is] the one great sight which every American should see.
>
> PRESIDENT THEODORE ROOSEVELT

The Rio Grande

The Rio Grande is another important river in the Southwest. Rio Grande means "big river" in Spanish. The Rio Grande flows almost 1,900 miles from the Rocky Mountains, across New Mexico, and forms the border between Texas and Mexico. Much of its water is used by farms along the way.

QUICK CHECK

Cause and Effect **How did the Grand Canyon form?**

D THE PROBLEM OF WATER

Citizenship
Be Informed

Natalie wanted to learn more about water resources. She watched a television program about Sandia Laboratory in New Mexico. Scientists there are finding ways to desalinate ocean water, or to turn ocean water into freshwater by taking the salt out of it. Natalie decided to write to Sandia Laboratory to find out more about how this process worked.

Write About It Research how desalination works. Write a report explaining why freshwater is an important resource.

The Southwest is the driest region of the United States. In some places, such as in the Sonoran Desert in Arizona, it rains as little as three inches a year. Because there is so little rain, having enough water is always a big concern.

The grasslands of Oklahoma and Texas normally get enough rain for prairie grasses to grow, but in some years there can be a **drought**. A drought is a long period of time with little or no rain. There was a drought during the 1930s. The crops died and the soil was so dry it turned to dust. The winds whipped up the dust and blew it in great drifts. The area became known as the Dust Bowl. Thousands of farmers had to sell their farms and leave the area.

Underground Water

Much of the water used for drinking and for watering crops in the Midwest and Southwest now comes from the Ogallala **Aquifer**. An aquifer is an underground area of rock, sand, or gravel that contains water. Aquifers formed thousands of years ago from streams, rivers, and melting glaciers. They are a renewable resource. Sometimes, however, people use a lot of water, and there is not enough rainfall to refill the aquifers. Then we have a shortage of water.

QUICK CHECK

Summarize **What are the problems with water in the Southwest?**

Rain in the Southwest usually comes in the form of afternoon thunderstorms.

Check Understanding

1. **VOCABULARY** Draw a picture of each vocabulary word.

   mesa   butte   canyon

2. **READING SKILL Cause and Effect** Use your chart from page 230 to write about what would happen to the water supply if the aquifers in the Southwest were emptied.

Cause	→	Effect
	→	
	→	
	→	

 EXPLORE The Big Idea

3. **Write About It** Write a paragraph about challenges that the geography and climate of the Southwest cause for people living there.

Map and Globe Skills
Use Special Purpose Maps: Population Maps

VOCABULARY

population density

population distribution

When you need to know the number of people who live in a place, you can look at a population map. Most population maps show population density. **Population density** measures how many people live in a certain area. The populations might be shown by state, county, or smaller areas.

Another kind of population map shows **population distribution**. This kind of map shows you where in an area people live. Look at the maps on the next page.

Learn It

- Map A is a population density map. On this map, the different colors stand for different population densities per square mile or square kilometer.

- The map key in Map A shows the number of people per square mile that each color represents. The color orange shows that between 15 and 99 people per square mile live in the areas that are shaded orange. Which color stands for the most people per square mile?

- Map B is a population distribution map.

- The map key in Map B shows that each dot stands for 50,000 people. By looking at where the dots are closest together, you can see where the most people live. In some places there are so many people that the dots run together.

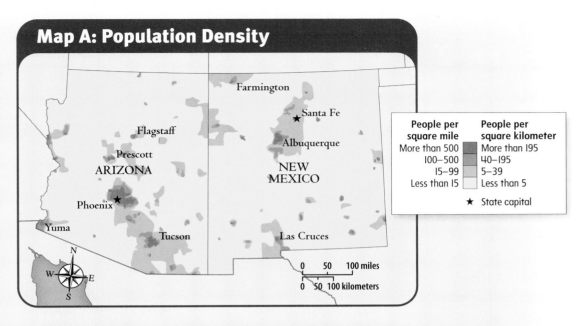

Map A: Population Density

Farmington

Santa Fe ★

Flagstaff

Albuquerque

Prescott

ARIZONA

NEW MEXICO

Phoenix ★

Yuma

Tucson

Las Cruces

People per square mile	People per square kilometer
More than 500	More than 195
100–500	40–195
15–99	5–39
Less than 15	Less than 5

★ State capital

0 50 100 miles
0 50 100 kilometers

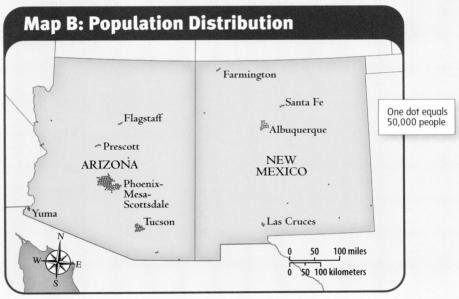

Map B: Population Distribution

Farmington

Santa Fe

Flagstaff

Albuquerque

Prescott

ARIZONA

NEW MEXICO

Phoenix-Mesa-Scottsdale

Yuma

Tucson

Las Cruces

One dot equals 50,000 people

0 50 100 miles
0 50 100 kilometers

Try It

Look at the maps. Then answer the questions.

- What does the color yellow mean in the key for Map A?

- Find New Mexico on Map B. Which city in New Mexico has the largest population?

Apply It

Look at the maps. Then answer the questions.

- What does Map B tell you that Map A does not?

- Which state has more people, Arizona or New Mexico?

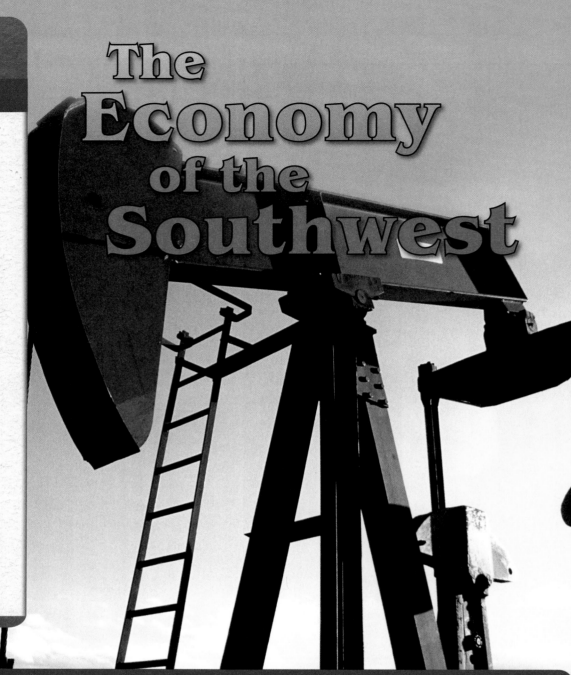

Lesson 2

VOCABULARY

kerosene p. 241

irrigation p. 242

silicon p. 244

solar energy p. 244

READING SKILL

Cause and Effect
Copy the chart. As you read, fill it in with information about the economy of the Southwest.

Cause	→	Effect
	→	
	→	
	→	

STANDARDS FOCUS

SOCIAL STUDIES Science, Technology, and Society

GEOGRAPHY Environment and Society

The Economy of the Southwest

Visual Preview

How do people in the Southwest use natural resources?

A Oil, minerals and cattle are natural resources of the Southwest.

AZ NM

B Growing crops and grazing animals are important in the Southwest.

C Many people in the Southwest work in technology.

A UNDERGROUND RESOURCES

If you flew over Oklahoma and Texas, you would see hundreds of oil wells. Every day, these wells pump up the Southwest's most valuable resource—petroleum.

Most petroleum is found deep underground. In the 1850s, petroleum was hard to get. People used it to make **kerosene**, a fuel oil burned in lamps and heaters. Then someone discovered that oil could be pumped to the surface through wells drilled in the ground.

Almost overnight, land that contained petroleum became extremely valuable. People throughout the region began to drill oil wells. Today the oil industry provides many jobs in the Southwest. Petroleum is used to make heating oil, gasoline, paints, and plastics.

EVENT

In 1901, **oil was found** in Spindletop, Texas. The new oil well produced over 75,000 barrels a day.

Spindletop

Mines and Metals

Gold, silver, and copper are all metals found in the Southwest. Use the map below to learn where to find other resources of the Southwest.

QUICK CHECK

Cause and Effect **What happened after underground petroleum was discovered?**

Products of the Southwest

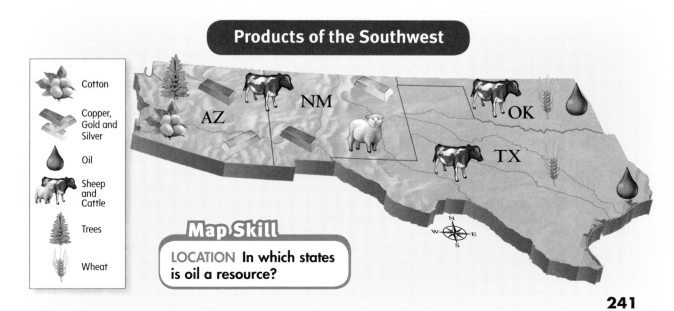

Cotton

Copper, Gold and Silver

Oil

Sheep and Cattle

Trees

Wheat

Map Skill

LOCATION In which states is oil a resource?

B FIELDS OF PLENTY

Not every resource in the Southwest is underground. If you drove through the Southwest, you would see mile after mile of farmland. The crops you see growing will vary depending on where you are.

Sugar cane and rice grow along the Gulf Coast in Texas where there is plenty of rain. In Oklahoma and Texas, farmers grow wheat and barley. Vegetables such as potatoes, cauliflower, broccoli, and lettuce are also grown in the Southwest.

In the 1830s and 1840s, many farmers moved from the Southeast to the Southwest to grow cotton. Today cotton is grown in all four southwestern states.

Because the Southwest is a dry region, farmers sometimes have a problem getting enough water. Some farmers use **irrigation** to grow crops. Irrigation is using pipes or ditches to bring water to fields. Many residents worry that the region's limited resources cannot provide enough water for everyone to use. Using water for irrigation has caused conflicts between farmers, Native Americans, and city residents.

This Navajo woman herds sheep in Arizona.

Cotton grows in all four states in the Southwest.

cotton

Grazing Fields

The plains of Oklahoma and Texas are dry. They do not have enough water for trees, but grass grows well there. Buffalo once roamed over this land and ate the grass. Today the grassy plains feed sheep and cattle.

chili peppers

Cattle came to the Southwest with Spanish settlers who started the region's first ranches. Later many African Americans, Native Americans, and whites worked together as cowboys in the Southwest.

You can still find cattle and sheep ranches across the Southwest. Texas leads the nation in producing beef cattle. Think of Southwest cattle next time you eat a hamburger!

QUICK CHECK

Make Generalizations Why is the Southwest a good place for cattle ranches?

Chili peppers grow in this irrigated field in Mesilla Valley in New Mexico.

Cowboys work on cattle ranches across the Southwest.

C TECHNOLOGY

Have you used a computer or cell phone lately? The chip in your computer or cell phone may have come from the Southwest. Texas, Arizona, and Oklahoma are all known for their computer technology industries.

New Mexico has worked hard to get technology companies to move there. New Mexico governor Bill Richardson said:

❝Technology-based economic development builds on some of New Mexico's greatest strengths in science, research and technology. . . .❞

Today, central New Mexico is home to a large computer industry. The nickname for this area is **"silicon** mesa." Silicon is a natural material that is found in rocks and sand. It is used to make computer chips. Did you notice a landform of the Southwest in the nickname?

Another important technology is the development of new sources of energy. One of these is **solar energy**, or energy that comes from the Sun. Solar energy is collected when sunlight hits solar panels. The Sun shines a lot in New Mexico, which makes it the perfect place for research into solar energy.

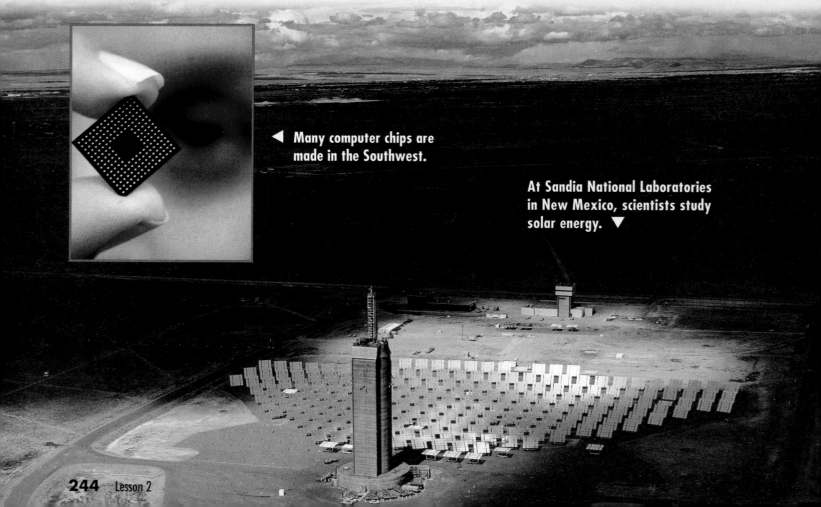

◀ Many computer chips are made in the Southwest.

At Sandia National Laboratories in New Mexico, scientists study solar energy. ▼

Ships and Spaceships

Texas has a long coast on the Gulf of Mexico. The Gulf ports of Houston, Texas, and Galveston, Texas, are major centers for shipping oil and other goods.

Another kind of ship is important in Houston, too—the space ship! Houston is the location of the Johnson Space Center, where part of our country's space program is located.

Because of its clear skies and dry climate, the Southwest is a good place for telescopes. Scientists use these telescopes to gather data about the stars and learn more about outer space.

QUICK CHECK

Summarize **What different technology industries exist in the Southwest?**

Astronaut Leroy Chiao trains in a pool at NASA's Johnson Space Center in Houston, Texas. ▼

Check Understanding

1. **VOCABULARY** Write a sentence for each vocabulary word.
   kerosene   irrigation   silicon

2. **READING SKILL Cause and Effect** Use the chart from page 240 to write about how the climate affects agriculture in the Southwest.

Cause	→	Effect
	→	
	→	
	→	

EXPLORE The Big Idea

3. **Write About It** Write a paragraph about how new technologies have helped the Southwest grow.

THE PEOPLE OF THE SOUTHWEST

Lesson 3

VOCABULARY
pueblo p. 247
adobe p. 247
powwow p. 252

READING SKILL
Cause and Effect
Copy the chart. As you read, fill it in with information about why different people have moved to the Southwest.

Cause	→	Effect
	→	
	→	
	→	

STANDARDS FOCUS

SOCIAL STUDIES Culture

GEOGRAPHY The Uses of Geography

Taos Pueblo in New Mexico

Visual Preview

How does the culture of a people affect their region?

A Native American groups include the Navajo, Hopi, and Pueblo people.

B Many people in the Southwest have Spanish or Mexican heritage.

C Immigrants and older Americans are moving to the Southwest today.

D People in the Southwest celebrate their culture in festivals.

A MYSTERY

Although Chaco Canyon is quiet now, many people lived there over 1,000 years ago. Who were these people? Where did they go?

Long ago, the people called the Ancestral Pueblo lived in Chaco Canyon. **Pueblo** is the Spanish word for village, and the Spanish use it to describe both the people and their homes. The Ancestral Pueblo built their homes along the steep sides of cliffs. They were built of **adobe**, a sun-baked clay brick. The pueblo in Chaco Canyon was once the center of trade and culture for the Ancestral Pueblo. It was home to about 1,000 people.

About 700 years ago, the Ancestral Pueblo left behind their cliff buildings, pueblos, and the beautiful pottery that they made. They settled in other parts of the Southwest. Today's Zuni, Hopi, and other Pueblo people are the descendents of the Ancestral Pueblo.

Some Pueblo people still live in pueblos today. The people of Acoma Pueblo in northwest New Mexico say that people have lived there for more than 700 years. That makes it the oldest continuously lived-in community in North America.

PEOPLE

After the Spanish introduced sheep to the Southwest, **Navajo weavers** used the sheep's wool to make beautiful blankets and rugs. The Navajo are still famous for their weaving.

Navajo weaver

The Navajo

Between 500 and 1,000 years ago, the Navajo (or Diné) came to the Southwest from farther north. At first the Navajo lived by hunting and growing corn.

The Spanish arrived in the 1500s and brought sheep to the region. The Navajo soon learned how to raise large herds of sheep.

Today many Native Americans of the Southwest live on reservations. In fact the Navajo reservation is the largest reservation in the United States. It covers parts of three states.

QUICK CHECK

Cause and Effect **How did Navajo life change after the Spanish brought sheep?**

B EUROPEANS IN THE SOUTHWEST

The first Europeans to explore the Southwest were the Spanish. Some, like Francisco de Coronado, came looking for gold. He came in 1540 with nearly 300 soldiers. The Spanish had heard stories of seven cities of gold and were eager to claim such a prize.

Coronado trekked as far as Kansas before he gave up. He found no gold, but he claimed many lands for Spain.

Some European explorers brought people from Africa to be scouts or guides in the Southwest. One of these men was Estevanico, a man from the country of Morocco in North Africa.

Spanish Settlements

Before the Pilgrims landed on Plymouth Rock, the Spanish had already built several settlements in the Southwest. One of their earliest settlements, Santa Fe, was founded in 1607 in the area that would become New Mexico. It was one of the first European settlements in the United States. The Spanish would build many more settlements in the Southwest.

Signs of Spanish and Mexican heritage can still be seen in the Southwest. In some locations, such as San Antonio, Texas, and Santa Fe, New Mexico, the city names are Spanish. Many buildings in the Southwest

This church in Sorroco, New Mexico, was built between 1615 and 1626 in a Spanish style.

were built using Spanish styles. Today more than one out of every four people in the Southwest has either Spanish or Mexican heritage.

Other Settlers

Once the area became part of the United States, other settlers hurried to get there. Some came looking for silver, copper, and gold. Others came to farm or to raise cattle and sheep.

QUICK CHECK

Sequence **What happened to the lands that Coronado began to explore in 1540?**

Francisco de Coronado and his soldiers explored the Southwest. ▼

Primary Sources

The first Spanish explorer of the Southwest was Cabeza de Vaca. In 1537, he wrote in his journal about a statement made by local Native American people:

"[T]hey gave us to understand that, very far from there, was a province called Apalachen in which there was much gold."

Write About It Write a journal entry describing what Cabeza de Vaca saw as he explored the Southwest.

For many years, the Southwest had the fewest people of any region. In the early 1900s, artists began coming to Arizona and New Mexico. They came because of the region's natural beauty. Today the cities of Santa Fe and Taos in New Mexico are famous as centers for art. Artists there are often inspired by the art of the region's Native Americans.

The development of the automobile and the highways and roads that followed made it easier for people to travel across the Southwest. Roads also made it easier to ship goods. By 1911 Phoenix, Arizona, had its first paved street.

Another reason people moved to the Southwest was air conditioning. In 1911 Willis Carrier built the first air conditioner. Within 20 years, many buildings in the Southwest were cooled by air conditioning. This invention made

Georgia O'Keeffe painted scenes of the Southwest. ▲

it possible for more people to live year-round in the warm Southwestern climate.

Population Increases

People are still moving to the Southwest. Phoenix, Arizona, is the fastest growing city in the nation. Many newcomers to the region are immigrants from other countries, such as Mexico and Honduras.

◄ Tourists and residents walk around Santa Fe, New Mexico.

Other newcomers come from different regions of the United States. Many older Americans retire to the Southwest. Tourists visit the Southwest, too. They are attracted by the natural beauty, the area's history and culture, and the mild winter climate.

QUICK CHECK

Summarize **What things attract people to the Southwest today?**

DataGraphic
Population Growth

Study the graph and map. Then answer the questions that follow.

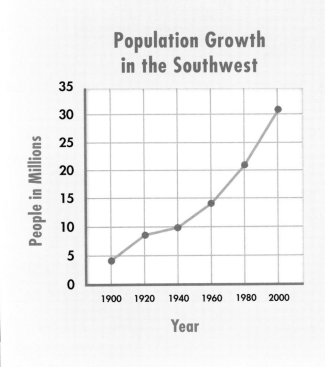

Population Growth in the Southwest

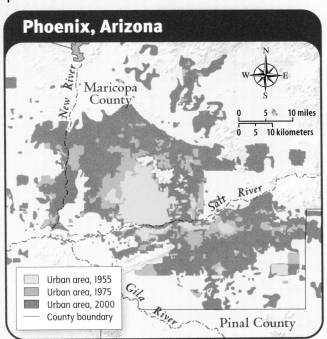

Phoenix, Arizona

Urban area, 1955
Urban area, 1975
Urban area, 2000
— County boundary

Think About Changes in Population

1. How has the size of the urban area of Phoenix, Arizona, changed since 1955?

2. What is the difference in the population between 1900 and 2000?

3. How are the data shown in the chart and in the map similar?

▲ These children are at a Native American powwow in New Mexico.

Ⓓ CELEBRATING CULTURE

Like the people of other regions, Southwesterners like to celebrate their heritage. Some attend **powwows**. A powwow is a Native American festival. What can you do at a powwow? You can see Native American dancing, listen to drummers, and taste fry bread, a delicious treat. One of the largest powwows in North America is held in Albuquerque, New Mexico, every spring.

Rain is important to Native Americans. Without enough rain, it is difficult to raise crops. The Hopi people pray to kachinas, or spirits, for rain. Every two years in August, dancers perform the Snake Dance to ask these spirits for rain.

EVENT

Every October, hot air balloons fill the skies at the **Albuquerque Balloon Fiesta** in Albuquerque, New Mexico.

Albuquerque Balloon Fiesta

This ceremony attracts thousands of visitors to Arizona.

Some festivals are held to celebrate local foods. In Crystal Beach, Texas, a Crab Festival is held every year. At the Hatch Chile Festival in Hatch, New Mexico, people can taste the chili peppers in many different recipes.

Still other festivals are just for fun. Albuquerque, New Mexico, has a hot-air balloon fiesta every October.

Historical Celebrations

Many people in the Southwest celebrate Cinco de Mayo, which means the "fifth of May" in Spanish. This Mexican holiday honors the Mexican army's victory over French soldiers at the Battle of Puebla in 1862.

March 2 is a state holiday in Texas. This holiday is called Texas Independence Day. On this day, people in Texas remember March 2, 1836. This was the day the settlers in Texas declared their independence from Mexico.

QUICK CHECK

Compare and Contrast **Describe the different celebrations in the Southwest.**

Check Understanding

1. **VOCABULARY** Write a sentence for each vocabulary word.
   pueblo　　**adobe**　　**powwow**

2. **READING SKILL Cause and Effect** Use the chart from page 246 to write about why the population of the Southwest has grown.

3. **Write About It** Write a paragraph about how Spanish settlers influenced the culture of the Southwest.

Cinco de Mayo is a Mexican holiday that is celebrated throughout the Southwest. ▼

Unit 6 Review and Assess

Vocabulary

Copy the sentences below. Use the vocabulary words to fill in the blanks.

adobe   **irrigation**

solar energy   **drought**

1. A farmer's entire crop could die if there is a _____ .

2. Many farmers in the Southwest depend on _____ for water.

3. Since New Mexico is sunny, it is a good place to study _____.

4. People in the Southwest use _____ bricks for building.

Comprehension and Critical Thinking

5. What natural resources are found in the Southwest?

6. To which countries did the states of the Southwest once belong?

7. **Critical Thinking** What makes grass important to the economy of the Southwest?

8. **Reading Skill** What is one cause of population growth in the Southwest?

Skill

Use Special Purpose Maps

Use the map to answer the questions.

9. Which county on the map has a population density of more than 1,000,000 people?

10. Which counties on the map have the second greatest population density?

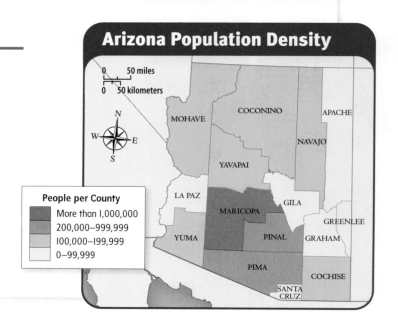

Arizona Population Density

0 50 miles

0 50 kilometers

People per County
- More than 1,000,000
- 200,000–999,999
- 100,000–199,999
- 0–99,999

MOHAVE, COCONINO, APACHE, NAVAJO, YAVAPAI, LA PAZ, GILA, MARICOPA, GREENLEE, YUMA, PINAL, GRAHAM, PIMA, COCHISE, SANTA CRUZ

Test Preparation

Read the paragraph. Then answer the questions.

The artist Georgia O'Keeffe especially loved the Southwest. Although she was not born there, she loved the landscape and the light in the region. She said it inspired her to do some of her best work. When asked why she liked Texas, for instance, she replied: "The openness. The dry landscape. The beauty of that wild world."

1. What is the main idea of this passage?

   A. Georgia O'Keeffe was a great artist.

   B. Texas has a very dry landscape.

   C. Georgia O'Keeffe loved the Southwest and thought it inspired some of her best work.

   D. Georgia O'Keeffe was not born in the Southwest.

2. Which statement best explains why the writer of the passage included a quote from Georgia O'Keeffe?

   A. The writer liked the sound of the quote.

   B. The writer liked New Mexico.

   C. The quote explains how O'Keeffe painted her pictures.

   D. The quote explains what O'Keeffe loved about the Southwest.

3. What inspired O'Keefe to do her best work?

   A. the landscape

   B. the landscape and the light

   C. the fact that she was born there

   D. the openness

4. Why might open, beautiful landscapes inspire an artist?

5. What else do you think might inspire an artist?

The Big Idea Activities

How do people adapt to their environment?

Write About the Big Idea

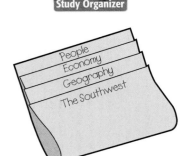
FOLDABLES™
Study Organizer

Expository Essay
In Unit 6, you read about the geography, economy, and people of the Southwest. Review the notes in the completed foldable. Begin with an introductory paragraph describing the environment in the Southwest. Then write a paragraph describing how the geography, economy, and people of the Southwest adapt to the environment. The final paragraph should summarize the main ideas of the essay.

Planning a Garden

Work independently to plan a xeriscape garden. A xeriscape garden contains plants that need very little water. Here's how to design your garden:

1. Do research to learn what xeriscape plants look like. Consider the height and color of the plants. Think about how much sunlight and water the plants need.

2. Choose several plants to use in your garden.

3. Draw a garden design that uses these plants.

4. Write an explanation of your plant selection and garden design.

5. Present your garden design to the class.

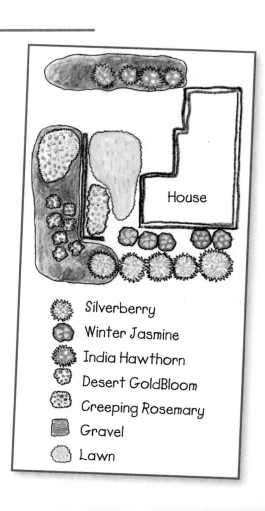

House

Silverberry
Winter Jasmine
India Hawthorn
Desert GoldBloom
Creeping Rosemary
Gravel
Lawn

The West

Unit 7

EXPLORE The Big Idea

Essential Question
How does technology change people's lives?

FOLDABLES Study Organizer

Make Generalizations
Use a three-tab book foldable to take notes as you read Unit 7. Label the three tabs **Geography**, **Economy**, and **People**.

LOG ON
For more about Unit 7 go to
www.macmillanmh.com

PEOPLE, PLACES, AND EVENTS

San Francisco

Chinatown–International District Summer Festival

New immigrants come to the United States each day. The Chinatown area of **San Francisco**, California, is home to many recent immigrants from Asia.

Today you can watch the **Chinatown–International District Summer Festival** in Seattle, Washington.

Jedediah Smith

The Rocky Mountains

In the early 1800s, trappers known as "mountain men" lived in **the Rocky Mountains** and hunted beavers for trade. Sometimes mountain men such as **Jedediah Smith** led pioneers across the mountains.

Today you can travel through Rocky Mountain National Park.

LOG ON

For more about People, Places, and Events, visit:
www.macmillanmh.com

Sutter's Mill in Sacramento, California

Miners

Gold was found at **Sutter's Mill in Sacramento, California**, in 1848. Between the late 1840s and the early 1860s, **miners** traveled throughout the West in search of gold.

Today you can visit Sutter's Mill in the Marshall Gold Discovery State Historic Park in California.

Volcanologists study Kilauea

Kilauea

Hawaii was formed by volcanoes. **Kilauea**, one of these volcanoes, is still erupting! **Volcanologists study Kilauea** to learn more about what causes volcanoes to erupt.

Today you can visit Kilauea and learn more about volcanoes.

West Region

1 The 605-foot Space Needle was built for the 1962 Seattle World's Fair.

People visit the cities, national parks, and ski resorts of the West.

HI

Kauai
Niihau
Oahu
Honolulu ★
Molokai
Lanai
Kahoolawe
Maui
Hawaii

5

PACIFIC
OCEAN

0   100   200 miles
0   100   200 kilometers

N W E S

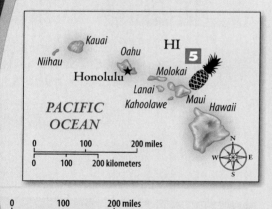

0   100   200 miles
0   100   200 kilometers

N W E S

5 Hawaiians wear different lei for different reasons. The most popular is the lei made of flowers.

GENERAL SHERMAN

6 Sequoia National Park is home to sequoias, the largest trees in the world.

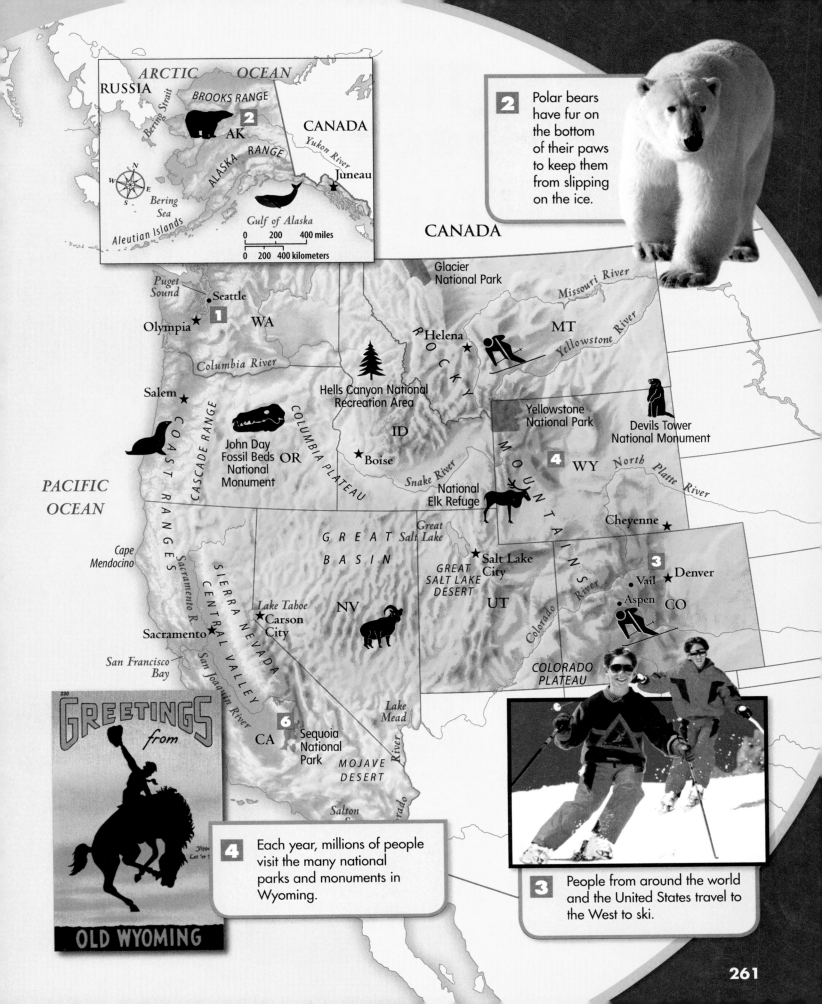

ARCTIC OCEAN

RUSSIA

BROOKS RANGE

CANADA

2

AK

ALASKA RANGE

Yukon River

Juneau

Bering Strait

Bering Sea

Aleutian Islands

Gulf of Alaska

N
W E
S

0   200   400 miles
0   200   400 kilometers

2 Polar bears have fur on the bottom of their paws to keep them from slipping on the ice.

CANADA

Puget Sound

Seattle

Olympia **1** WA

Glacier National Park

Missouri River

Columbia River

Helena MT Yellowstone River

ROCKY

Salem

Hells Canyon National Recreation Area

COAST RANGES

CASCADE RANGE

COLUMBIA PLATEAU

John Day Fossil Beds National Monument OR

ID

Boise

Snake River

Yellowstone National Park

Devils Tower National Monument

National Elk Refuge

4 WY

North Platte River

MOUNTAINS

PACIFIC OCEAN

Cape Mendocino

Sacramento R.

SIERRA NEVADA

CENTRAL VALLEY

GREAT BASIN

Great Salt Lake

Lake Tahoe
Carson City

NV

GREAT SALT LAKE DESERT

Salt Lake City

UT

Cheyenne

3

Colorado River

Vail
Aspen

Denver

CO

COLORADO PLATEAU

San Francisco Bay

Sacramento

San Joaquin River

6

CA

Sequoia National Park

Lake Mead

MOJAVE DESERT

Salton

230

GREETINGS from

Yippe Let 'er

OLD WYOMING

4 Each year, millions of people visit the many national parks and monuments in Wyoming.

3 People from around the world and the United States travel to the West to ski.

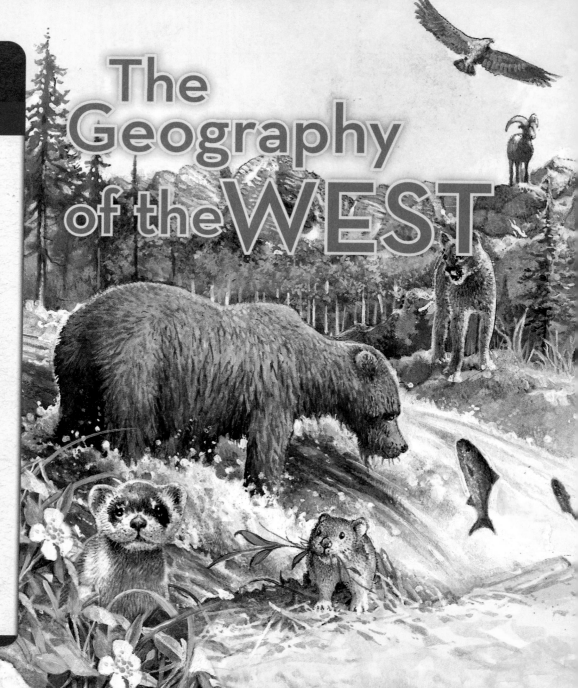

The Geography of the WEST

Lesson 1

VOCABULARY

earthquake p. 266

magma p. 266

geyser p. 267

timberline p. 268

READING SKILL

Make Generalizations
Copy the chart. As you read, fill it in with information about the mountains and rivers in the West.

Text Clues	What You Know	Generalizations

STANDARDS FOCUS

SOCIAL STUDIES: People, Places, and Environments

GEOGRAPHY: Physical Systems

Visual Preview

How has the geography of the West affected the way people live?

A The West is a land of extreme environments.

B The West has tall mountains and the Great Salt Lake.

C The West has earthquakes, volcanoes, and geysers.

D Elevation and latitude affect climate in the West.

Ⓐ A VAST REGION

Volcanoes, a tropical rain forest, hot deserts, bubbling mud flats, glaciers, and the country's tallest mountains make the West a land of extreme environments.

The West is the largest region of the United States. It contains eleven states. This region includes Hawaii, our only island state, and Alaska, our largest state. The West is a vast area, and as you might guess, the landforms and climates vary greatly.

Many Environments

The West has almost every landform and type of environment you can name. It includes landforms from snow-capped mountains to fiery volcanoes. The environments range from sun-baked deserts to thick forests that receive a huge amount of rain.

The many plants and animals of the region have adapted to the different environments. Animals such as bears and golden eagles live in forests and along the coast. Plants such as the blue columbine live in the Rocky Mountains, while the frangipani is native to Hawaii.

Plants and Animals of the West

Ponderosa Pine

Salmon

Quaking Aspen

Grizzly Bear

Rocky Mountain Blue Columbine

Golden Eagle

frangipani

bear

QUICK CHECK

Make Generalizations **How do plants and animals survive in different environments?**

MOUNTAINS AND WATERS

The Rocky Mountains are North America's largest mountain range. They stretch more than 3,000 miles from Alaska to New Mexico. At 14,433 feet high, Colorado's Mount Elbert is the highest mountain in the range.

The Rockies are young mountains—only 65 million years old. How did the Rocky Mountains form? Earth's surface is made up of huge plates. The plates float on an underground layer of warm, soft rock. The floating plates often bump together or grind into each other. Sometimes one plate slides under another plate and pushes the top plate up. The Rocky Mountains formed when two plates collided.

Rivers

The Rockies get a lot of snow. In some places, the winter snows start in August and don't melt until the following June. As this snow melts, rivers form. The Rio Grande, the Missouri, and the Colorado, as well as many tributaries, all have their sources in the Rocky Mountains.

◄ Melting snow runs downhill into this stream in the Colorado mountains.

The Great Salt Lake

The rivers and streams that flow into Utah's Great Salt Lake bring freshwater and about a million tons of salt each year. The hot summer sun evaporates the water, and salt is left behind. Since more and more water evaporates each year, the Great Salt Lake is shrinking.

Today the Great Salt Lake is saltier than the ocean. With all of that salt, swimmers can float easily.

The Great Salt Lake is too salty for fish, but plenty of shrimp live there. These shrimp attract many birds. Pelicans, ibis, and other birds visit the marshes along the lake's shores to feed on the shrimp.

QUICK CHECK

Cause and Effect What forces formed the Rocky Mountains?

This white-faced ibis looks for food in the Great Salt Lake. ▶

The Great Salt Lake is near the Wasatch Range of the Rocky Mountains.

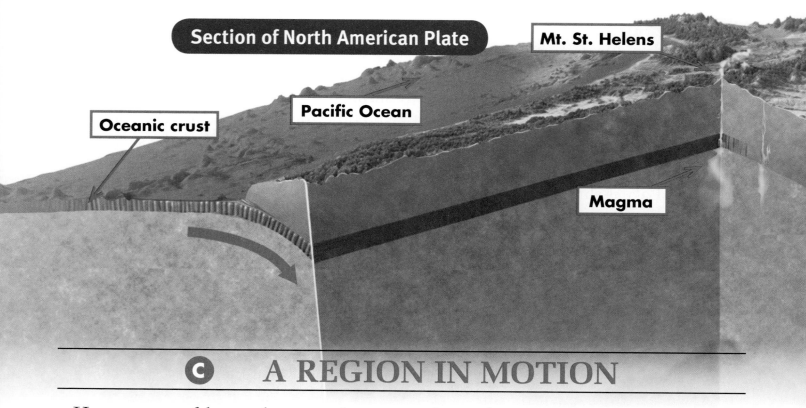

Section of North American Plate

Mt. St. Helens

Oceanic crust

Pacific Ocean

Magma

C A REGION IN MOTION

Have you ever felt your house or the ground shake from an **earthquake**? In a mild earthquake, the ground trembles and dishes rattle on shelves. During a powerful earthquake, buildings can fall down and large cracks appear in roads.

A powerful earthquake damaged houses in San Francisco, California. ▼

As you know, Earth's surface is made up of plates. The movement of one plate against another can cause earthquakes. The Pacific coast, the region's border, is one place where plates push together. Earthquakes occur frequently along the coast.

Volcanoes

Magma, or underground melted rock, may push through openings that are made as plates move. When magma reaches Earth's surface, it is called lava. Sometimes volcanoes erupt violently and throw lava, hot ash, or gases into the air. Mount St. Helens, in Washington, erupted with a huge explosion in 1980. Other volcanoes, such as Kilauea, in Hawaii, allow lava and gases to flow quietly out of cracks in the ground.

Cascades

Continental Divide

Yellowstone

Continental Crust

Diagram Skill

Where does magma reach the surface?

Magma

Hot Spots

Some volcanoes form from hot spots, or places in the middle of a plate where magma reaches Earth's surface. Yellowstone National Park is a giant collapsed volcano that formed from a hot spot. Although the volcano last erupted about 600,000 years ago, the heat from the magma still causes mud to bubble. It warms water in springs and shoots steam and water into the air.

Hot springs are bodies of water that are heated by magma. Sometimes, the underground water gets so hot it turns to steam. The pressure from the steam builds up until a **geyser** occurs. A geyser is a hot spring that occasionally shoots hot water or steam into the air.

PLACES

Old Faithful is the most famous geyser in Yellowstone. It sends up 100-foot sprays of water about every hour.

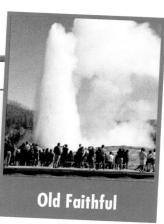

Old Faithful

The Hawaiian islands formed because of a hot spot underneath the Pacific Ocean. Lava from this hot spot formed volcanoes on the ocean floor. Over time, these volcanoes grew larger and reached the surface. Since some of the volcanoes still erupt, the islands continue to grow.

QUICK CHECK

Cause and Effect **What causes an earthquake?**

You can see the timberline on these mountains in the John Muir Wilderness Area in California.

...I have walked ... up in the higher piney ... scented forests of the cool mountains.

—JOHN MUIR

D CLIMATE IN THE WEST

You already know that the higher up a mountain you go, the colder it gets. Another way to say this is to say that elevation affects climate.

If you hike in the Rockies, you can see and feel the change in temperature. The valleys are covered with forest, but as you climb higher, the trees are shorter and there are fewer of them. Finally, you reach an elevation where it is too cold for trees to grow. This is called the **timberline**, or tree line. Instead of trees, there are stretches of grass and low-growing plants.

Did you know that Hawaii has mountains? Many of the mountains are volcanos. A few of them are so high that it is cold enough for snow to fall on the mountaintops.

Latitude and Climate

If you have ever heard someone say, "This place feels like the North Pole!" you know that means it's really cold. The closer a location is to either the North Pole or the South Pole, the colder the temperature. The latitude of a place, or how close or far a place is to the equator, affects climate.

For example, Alaska is the most northern state in the United States. It is far away from the equator. Alaska has cool summers and very cold winters. During the summer, temperatures may reach 80 degrees Fahrenheit. In the winter, the temperature can become colder than 60 degrees below zero.

Latitudes nearer the equator are warmer. Hawaii's latitude is closer to the equator. Although Hawaii's mountain-tops get snow, most of Hawaii has a warm, tropical climate.

Precipitation

The Olympic Peninsula in Washington is the wettest area in the United States, not counting Hawaii. This area receives as much as 160 inches of rain every year. Some plants and animals that live in this area are found nowhere else in the world. They grow well in the heavy precipitation and mild climate.

What effect does a mountain range have on precipitation? The areas on the western side of the Rocky Mountains receive a lot of rain. The eastern areas are in the rain shadow of the Rocky Mountains and receive very little rain.

QUICK CHECK

Compare and Contrast **How are the climates of Alaska and Hawaii different?**

The plants that grow on the Olympic Peninsula in Washington are similar to plants that grow near the equator. ▼

Check Understanding

1. **VOCABULARY** Draw a picture of each vocabulary word.

   earthquake   magma
   geyser   timberline

2. **READING SKILL** Make Generalizations Use the chart from page 262 to write about the climate in the Rocky Mountains.

Text Clues	What You Know	Generalization

3. **Write About It** Write a paragraph about how the geography of the West may cause challenges to people who live there.

Map and Globe Skills

Use Road Maps

VOCABULARY

interstate
  highway

road map

There are thousands of roads in our country. Some roads follow the paths that Native Americans or early settlers used. Other roads, such as interstate highways, were planned. An **interstate highway** has two or more lanes and goes across two or more states.

A **road map** shows where the roads go in a certain area. By reading a road map, you can figure out how to travel from one place to another.

Learn It

- The map of Montana's highways on page 271 shows several different types of highways. Each highway is known by a number and a symbol.

- In most cases, odd-numbered highways run north and south, and even-numbered highways run east and west. This numbering system helps drivers figure out which road to take.

- The symbol with double red lines behind a red and blue shield represents interstate highways. Interstate highways are usually fast roads that have on- and off-ramps and do not have traffic lights.

- The symbol for U.S. highways is one red line behind a white shield. These highways often pass through town centers.

- A black line behind a white oval is the symbol for a state highway. State highways run only within a state.

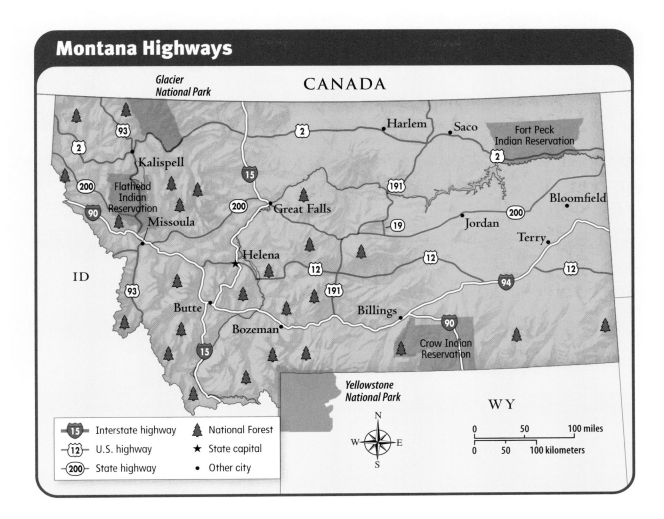

Montana Highways

Glacier National Park · CANADA · Harlem · Saco · Fort Peck Indian Reservation · Kalispell · Flathead Indian Reservation · Great Falls · Bloomfield · Missoula · Jordan · Terry · Helena · ID · Butte · Billings · Bozeman · Crow Indian Reservation · Yellowstone National Park · WY

Legend:
- 15 Interstate highway
- 12 U.S. highway
- 200 State highway
- ▲ National Forest
- ★ State capital
- • Other city

0   50   100 miles
0   50   100 kilometers

Try It

● How is the direction of Interstate 15 different from Interstate 94?

● Which road would you take to get from Billings to Terry?

Apply It

● Which cities can you reach by traveling on state highway 2?

● Find a road map that shows your state. What roads are near where you live?

Lesson 2

The ECONOMY of the WEST

VOCABULARY

telecommunications p. 276

conservationist p. 279

READING SKILL

Make Generalizations
Copy the chart. As you read, fill it in with information about natural resources and farming in the West.

Text Clues	What You Know	Generalization

STANDARDS FOCUS

SOCIAL STUDIES Production, Distribution, and Consumption

GEOGRAPHY The World in Spatial Terms

A dogsled travels past an oil pipeline near Wiseman, Alaska.

Visual Preview

How does technology change the economy of a region?

A Oil, lumber, and minerals are resources that provide many jobs in the West.

B Ranching and farming are important to the economy of the West.

C Movies and high-tech manufacturing are growing industries.

D Tourism is an important part of the economy of the West.

A NATURAL RESOURCES

Many settlers came to the West because of the rich natural resources. These natural resources are still providing jobs today.

When gold was discovered in California in 1848, word spread quickly. Thousands of people caught "gold fever" and rushed west to strike it rich. The same thing happened with silver in Nevada in 1859 and with gold in Alaska in 1898. Mining minerals is still an important part of the economy of many western states.

Energy resources are important, too. Wyoming's most important industry is the production of oil and natural gas. Wyoming is also the leading producer of uranium in the United States. Uranium is used to produce nuclear energy.

Alaskan Oil

What is made of metal, 800 miles long, and filled with oil? The Alaska pipeline, of course! When oil was discovered in northern Alaska in 1968, experts decided the best

way to transport the oil was by pipe. The pipeline was built to carry the oil from the Arctic to the ice-free port of Valdez. From there, ships carry the oil to refineries, where the oil is broken down into products such as gasoline.

QUICK CHECK

Make Generalizations **Why would it be useful to have oil in Alaska piped to an ice-free port?**

Logging is an important industry in western Montana, Idaho, Washington, and Oregon. ▶

Montana has huge deposits of copper ore. ▶

B   BY LAND AND SEA

As you have learned, the landforms in the West vary greatly. How does this affect the economy of the West? Some places are good for farming and for raising animals. In other places, people make a living by fishing. The products and industries in the West are as varied as the landscape itself.

QUICK CHECK

Summarize **How do the landforms in the West affect the economy?**

Have you ever seen a one-hundred-pound cabbage? Since Alaska is so far north, summer days can be 20 hours long. With all that sunlight, farmers in Alaska have grown cabbages that large!

Alaska has a coast more than 6,000 miles long, and leads the country in commercial fishing. Catching, harvesting, and canning seafood make food-processing Alaska's biggest industry.

Sugarcane and pineapples are grown in large fields in Hawaii. Cattle ranching is also important to the state's economy.

California has a valley running down the middle of the state called the Central Valley. This one valley produces more fruits, nuts, and vegetables than almost any place on Earth!

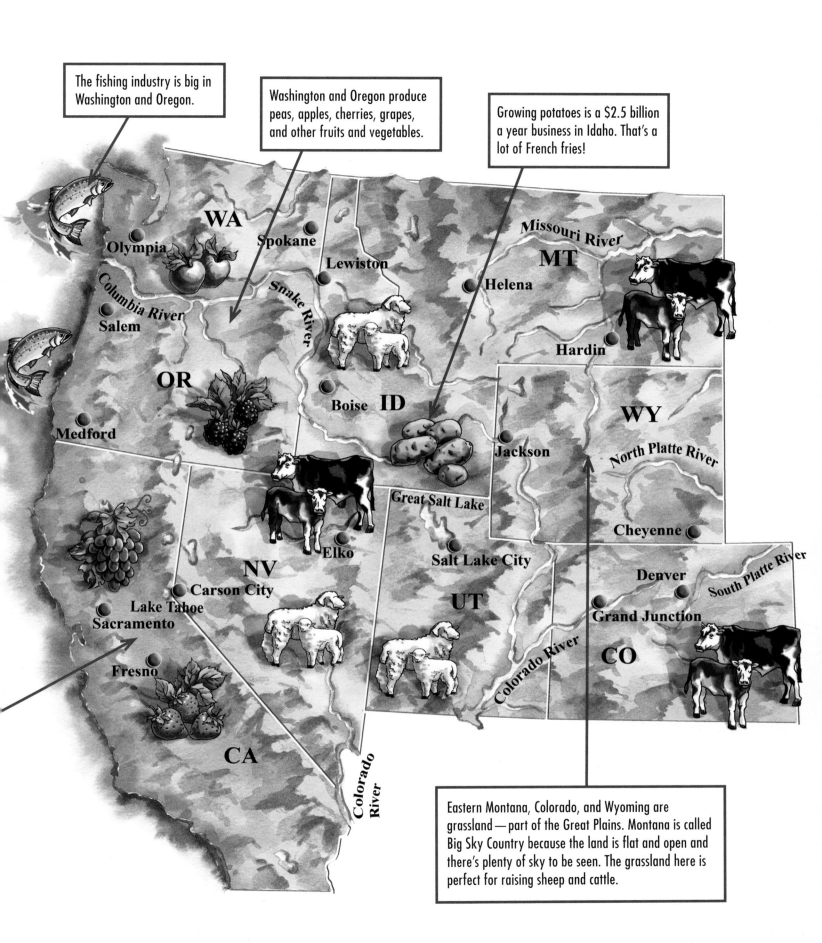

The fishing industry is big in Washington and Oregon.

Washington and Oregon produce peas, apples, cherries, grapes, and other fruits and vegetables.

Growing potatoes is a $2.5 billion a year business in Idaho. That's a lot of French fries!

Eastern Montana, Colorado, and Wyoming are grassland — part of the Great Plains. Montana is called Big Sky Country because the land is flat and open and there's plenty of sky to be seen. The grassland here is perfect for raising sheep and cattle.

WA
Olympia
Spokane
Columbia River
Salem
OR
Medford

Lewiston
Snake River
Boise   ID

Great Salt Lake

Missouri River
MT
Helena
Hardin

WY
North Platte River
Cheyenne

Jackson
Salt Lake City
UT

Denver
South Platte River
Grand Junction
CO
Colorado River

NV
Carson City
Lake Tahoe
Sacramento
Fresno
Elko

CA
Colorado River

MAKING IT OUT WEST

The economy of the West depends on natural resources and farming. It also depends on industries that make technology and on the federal government.

Some of the West's natural resources are used to make goods. Pencils, baseball bats, lumber for houses, and a thousand other things are manufactured from trees that grow in Western forests.

Hollywood, California, is famous for a special industry. Can you guess what it is? The movie business, of course! The movie industry employs hundreds of other people besides the stars you see on the screen. These people write the stories, create scenery and costumes, style hair, and put on make-up. They also work cameras, create computerized special effects, and do many other jobs that need to be done in order for a movie to be finished.

The movies produced in Hollywood include *Pirates of the Caribbean: Dead Man's Chest.*

Technology

The area around San Jose and Santa Clara in California is famous for another big industry—computers. The area's nickname is Silicon Valley, named for the natural material used to make computer chips. Companies in Washington and Utah are leaders in the manufacturing of computers and other high-tech equipment.

Today many people use cell phones. Cell phones depend on **telecommunications**, or the technology that lets people send messages and images over long distances. Many people in the West work in the telecommunications industry.

◄ New car designs are often tested at the Bonneville Salt Flats, a desert in northwest Utah.

Federal Government

The federal government is a big employer in the West. In Hawaii, for example, one in ten people are either members of the army or navy or family members of someone in the military.

Almost two-thirds of the land in Utah and more than three-quarters of the land in Nevada is owned by our federal government. The flat deserts are perfect places for testing fast cars, planes, and missiles. Military pilots learn to fly at military bases located throughout the West.

The federal government is the top customer of companies in Utah that manufacture rocket engines. The government also supports scientific research in the West, including monitoring earthquakes and volcanoes and sending robot exploration devices into space.

Citizenship

Volunteering

In 1989 an oil tanker spilled 11 million gallons of oil into the ocean off the coast of Alaska. The oil stuck to the feathers and fur of thousands of animals and contaminated miles of Alaska shoreline. Volunteers caught and cleaned the dirty animals and washed the shoreline.

Write About It Write a paragraph explaining ways students can help protect the environment.

QUICK CHECK

Make Inferences **What makes a flat desert a perfect place to test cars or rockets?**

277

Global Connections

International Trade

International trade happens when countries buy and sell each other's goods. Why would people buy goods made in another country? Sometimes the goods may be natural resources or products that people in that country don't have. Sometimes goods can be made more cheaply in one country.

Bicycles can be made more cheaply in China than in the United States, for example. In 1990 about six times more bicycles were made in China than in the United States. More stores wanted to buy bicycles from China because they were less expensive. By 2000, companies in China made fifty-two times more bicycles than companies in the United States.

China

United States

▲ Workers in China make bicycles.

▲ Families in the United States buy bicycles.

Remember all that awesome scenery you read about? It brings lots of visitors to the West. In winter, people grab skis and snowboards and hit the snowy slopes of the mountains. In summer, tourists explore the wilderness on foot or on horseback. Tourists also enjoy the beaches in California and Hawaii.

What do all of these vacationing people have to do with jobs? Think of all the things tourists need or want, from hotel rooms to restaurants to tour guides. Tourism provides lots of jobs. In some places, entire towns have sprung up to serve the needs of tourists.

Park rangers teach visitors about the animals and plants in the national parks.

National Parks

Many of the most beautiful places in the West have been set aside forever as national parks. These parks were the work of **conservationists**, or people who want to protect wilderness and wildlife. Each year, thousands of people visit the many National Parks in the West.

QUICK CHECK

Main Idea and Details **Why is tourism important to the economy of the West?**

Check Understanding

1. **VOCABULARY** Write a sentence for each vocabulary word.

   telecommunications   **conservationist**

2. **READING SKILL** Make Generalizations Use the chart from page 272 to write about the service jobs in the West.

Text Clues	What You Know	Generalization

3. **Write About It** Write a sentence about how tourism creates jobs in the West.

279

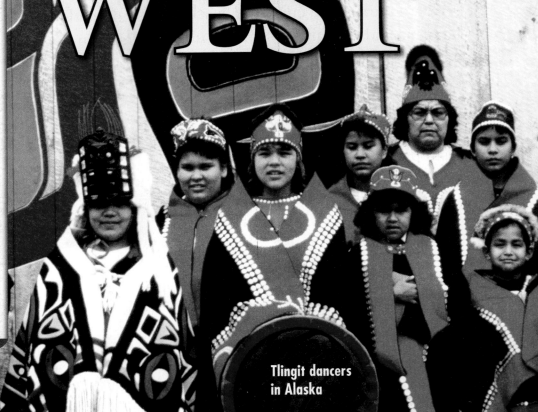

Lesson 3

VOCABULARY

bison p. 281

rodeo p. 285

READING SKILL

Make Generalizations
Copy the chart. As you read, fill it in with information about the people who have lived in the West.

Text Clues	What You Know	Generalizations

STANDARDS FOCUS

SOCIAL STUDIES Individuals, Groups, and Institutions

GEOGRAPHY The Uses of Geography

THE PEOPLE of the WEST

Tlingit dancers in Alaska

Visual Preview

How has the culture of the West changed over time?

A The West is home to many Native Americans.

B People from around the world have come to the West.

C The West has interesting cities, events, and festivals.

280

LIVING IN THE WEST

Today there are people from every continent living in the eleven states of the West. First, though, there were the Native Americans.

You have learned that the West has many different environments, from forests to grasslands to deserts. The Native Americans who lived in these different environments had different ways of life.

Some Native Americans hunted, fished, and gathered food in the mountains and moved with the seasons. They often joined the Plains Indians to hunt antelope or **bison**. Most people call the bison a buffalo. A bison is a large, shaggy animal.

Along the Pacific coast, the people lived in villages near the ocean. They fished for salmon in the ocean and in rivers, and built sturdy homes of cedarwood. Further north, the Inuit survived in the icy Arctic by hunting and fishing. The people who first settled Hawaii came from the South Pacific islands about 1,000 years ago.

Native Americans Today

Many Native Americans still live in the West. Some live on reservations and others live in towns and cities. Native American groups such as the Lakota continue to teach their art and language to children and adults.

QUICK CHECK

Make Generalizations How did Native American foods depend on their location?

Kevin Red Star is a Native American artist who paints images of historical and modern Crow culture. ▼

Ⓑ WESTWARD HO!

People have been heading to the West for many years. The Spanish settled throughout California and the Southwest. Later, fur trappers known as "mountain men" led people heading west through the dangerous Rocky Mountains.

In the 1830s and 1840s, settlers who wanted rich farmlands in Oregon began traveling west by wagon train. In the late 1840s, Asian immigrants came to mine for gold. Around 1879 many African Americans called Exodusters moved west to find freedom from unfair treatment.

When the first railroad to cross the continent was finished in 1869, more and more people began moving west. In the early 1900s, the invention of the automobile made travel to the West even easier.

PEOPLE

Dorothea Lange became famous when she photographed Dust Bowl farmers who migrated to California in the 1930s.

Dorothea Lange

Spanish settlers built missions and raised cattle.

Chinese workers came to mine for gold. Many stayed to work on the railroads.

The West Today

The West is one of our nation's fastest-growing regions. The population of Nevada alone doubled between 1990 and 2004. Immigrants have come from all over, but especially from Asian countries such as Japan, China, India, and Vietnam.

Seema Handu, a scientist who moved to California from India, said,

" . . . I always wanted to come to the United States to study and do research . . . . There are so many opportunities here. **"**

QUICK CHECK

Summarize **What events caused people to move to the West?**

Primary Sources

[This country] has assuredly the most healthy climate in the world . . . Any [one] . . . would be satisfied.

From a letter written by Oregon settler Isaac Statt, 1847

Write About It Write about how the climate of your area affects the crops grown there.

In the 1930s, many families traveled from the Midwest to the West to escape the Dust Bowl.

Many Asian immigrants now work in the West.

This tiger float was part of the Rose Festival parade in Portland, Oregon.

C SIGHTS AND CELEBRATIONS

Many people come to the West to see its wide-open spaces and breathtaking scenery. The West also has big cities and celebrations that attract visitors.

People from around the world visit the hotels and shows in Las Vegas, Nevada. Seattle, Washington, has a tower called the Space Needle. You can ride an elevator to its restaurant, which is 520 feet, or about 43 stories, above the city.

In California, travelers visit San Francisco's Chinatown and the Golden Gate Bridge. Theme parks and Hollywood bring visitors to Los Angeles.

Portland, Oregon, is another beautiful Western city. Each year, more than half a million people visit Portland for the Rose Festival. They watch a parade and enjoy the floats, carnivals, boat races, music, and, of course, roses!

EVENT

In Alaska's **Iditarod** race, dogsled drivers take an average of 10 days to drive teams of dogs over a thousand miles of snow!

Iditarod

Ride 'em Cowboy!

What's the West without a **rodeo**? Rodeos are shows that have contests in horseback riding, roping, and other similar skills. Rodeos were started as a way to celebrate cowboy skills. One favorite event is bull riding. Cowboys climb onto the back of a 2,000-pound bull, hold on with just one hand, and try to stay on for eight seconds. Another event is steer wrestling, in which a cowboy on horseback chases and ropes a steer, then jumps off the horse and wrestles the steer to the ground. Finally he ties its legs together. Whoever does all this in the fastest time wins!

Crow Festival

One of the largest Native American festivals in the nation is held each year in Crow Agency, Montana. Native Americans and visitors come from all over the West. They set up more than 1,500 teepees along the banks of the Little Bighorn River. You can listen to drum groups and watch dances.

QUICK CHECK

Summarize **Why do visitors come to the West?**

Children try to pull ribbons off a calf during the calf scramble event at a rodeo in Gardiner, Montana. ▼

Check Understanding

1. **VOCABULARY** Write a sentence for each vocabulary word.
   bison   **rodeo**

2. **READING SKILL** Make Generalizations Use the chart from page 280 to write about the sights and celebrations in the West.

Text Clues	What You Know	Generalizations

3. **EXPLORE The Big Idea** **Write About It** Write a paragraph about how changes in technology affected how people traveled to the West.

Unit 7 Review and Assess

Vocabulary

Copy the sentences below. Use the vocabulary words to fill in the blanks.

magma   **timberline**
conservationist   **rodeo**

1. Contests in riding and roping happen at a _____.

2. When liquid rock is underground, it is called _____.

3. The elevation where the temperature is too cold for trees to grow is called the _____.

4. A _____ works to preserve and protect the wilderness.

Comprehension and Critical Thinking

5. What nonrenewable resources are found in the West?

6. What are some of the crops grown in the West?

7. **Reading Skill** Which area of the West would you prefer to live in? Make generalizations to tell why.

8. **Critical Thinking** How do the different landforms of the West affect the kinds of jobs that people in those areas have?

Skill

Use Road Maps

Write a complete sentence to answer each question.

9. Which road would you take to travel from Salt Lake City to Cedar City?

10. Which interstate highways run near Fishlake National Forest?

Utah Road Map

- 15 Interstate highway   ★ State capital
- 40 U.S. highway   • Other city

ID
Wasatch-Cache National Forest
Great Salt Lake
84
15
84
80   80
Salt Lake City
Provo   40   191   Vernal
Nephi   6
NV   Price
6   6
6   15
70
CO
Fishlake National Forest
Cedar City   15   191
Bryce Canyon National Park
WY
0   50   100 miles
0   50   100 kilometers
N W E S
AZ   NM

Test Preparation

Read the paragraphs. Then answer the questions.

In 1869 Wyoming's government decided to let women vote in local elections. Wyoming was not yet a state, only a territory. At that time, no other part of the United States allowed women to vote.

Soon Colorado and Idaho let women vote in some elections, too. Other states did the same. Finally, in 1920, voters amended the Constitution to allow women to vote in all elections. Wyoming had led the way.

1. What would be a good title for this passage?

   A. All About Voting

   B. Women's Right to Vote

   C. The Constitution Changes

   D. Women in the Mountain States

2. According to the passage, which statement is true?

   A. Today, women are not permitted to vote in some states.

   B. The Constitution allowed women to vote as early as 1867.

   C. Idaho was the first territory in the United States to allow women to vote.

   D. After 1920, women could vote in all elections.

3. Which territory was the first to allow women to vote?

   A. Idaho

   B. Colorado

   C. Washington, D.C.

   D. Wyoming

4. Why do you think women were not allowed to vote before 1869?

5. Why do you think it took 51 years from the time women in Wyoming were allowed to vote for the Constitution to be changed to allow all women to vote?

The Big Idea Activities

How does technology change people's lives?

Write About the Big Idea

Expository Essay
In Unit 7, you read about the geography, economy, and people of the West. Review your notes in the completed foldable. Write a paragraph describing how the geography, economy, and people of the West use technology to change their lives. Begin with an introductory paragraph describing the environment in the Southeast. The final paragraph should summarize the main ideas of the essay.

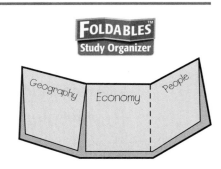

FOLDABLES™
Study Organizer

Geography Economy People

Living and Working in the West

Work in a small group to make a collage. The subject is living and working in the West. Here's how to make your collage:

1. Research how people in the West live and work.

2. Come up with ideas about what you want to show in your collage. Be sure to include examples of the landforms of the region.

3. Look through magazines for photos that show your ideas. Ask for permission before you cut out the photos.

4. Arrange your photos on a background so they tell a story about living and working in the West. Write a paragraph that describes the work your group has done.

5. Present your collage to the class.

Reference Section

The Reference Section has many parts, each with a different type of information. Use this section to look up people, places, and events as you study.

Unit 3 • Reading Skills
Main Idea and Details

In this unit you will learn about the land, economy, and culture of the Northeast. Thinking about the main idea and details will help you understand how and why the region has changed over time.

The main idea is what a paragraph is all about. Often it is the first sentence in a paragraph. The supporting details tell about, or support, the main idea.

Learn It

- Think about what a paragraph is all about.

- Decide whether the first sentence states the main idea.

- Look for details. Think about what these details tell about.

- Now read the paragraph below. Look for the main ideas and details.

Main Idea
The first sentence states the main idea.

Details
These details tell where most of the energy comes from.

The Northeast's energy comes from different sources. Oil and gas supply much of the region's power. The Northeast also uses water power to produce energy. Hot water and steam from deep underground also provide energy in parts of the region.

Try It

Copy the chart below. Then fill in the chart with the main idea and details from the paragraph on page R6.

Main Idea	Details

How did you find the main idea and supporting details?

Apply It

● Review the steps for finding the main idea and details in Learn It.

● Now read the paragraph below. Make a chart to show the main idea and supporting details.

In the late 1700s, some people in England learned how to build machines that wove lots of cloth all at once. These machines ran on water power. As you learned in the last lesson, the Northeast has plenty of water power. By the middle 1700s, many settlers were using the region's rivers and falls to run mills that turned grain into flour.

Unit 4 • Reading Skills

Summarize

In this unit you will learn about the Southeast. Learning how to summarize, or stating the important ideas in a reading passage, will help you remember what you learned. A summary gives the main ideas, but leaves out minor details. Summarizing will help you understand and remember what you read.

Learn It

- Find the main ideas in a passage. Restate these important points briefly.
- Find important details and combine them in your summary.
- Leave out details that are not important.
- Now read the passage below and think about how you would summarize it.

Main Topic
This is the main topic of the paragraph.

Supporting Facts
These facts support the main topic.

There are many rivers in the Southeast, but the Mississippi River is one of the largest. The writer Mark Twain called it "the majestic, the magnificent Mississippi." The river flows 2,350 miles from Minnesota to the Gulf of Mexico in Louisiana. As it flows south, it carries 400 million tons of silt and mud. All this silt and mud gets dumped at the river's mouth to make a landform known as the Mississippi Delta.

Copy the chart below. Then fill in the chart with your conclusions from the paragraph on page R8.

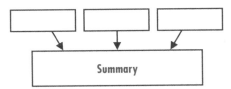

What did you look for to summarize the paragraph?

Apply It

- Review the steps for summarizing in Learn It.
- Read the passage below. Then summarize the passage using a summary chart.

The Southeast has hundreds of islands. Some were formed by ocean waves that dropped tons of sand along the coast. Others were made from the bones of millions and millions of coral, a tiny sea animal.

The largest island of the Southeast is Puerto Rico, in the Caribbean Sea. It was formed millions of years ago by the action of volcanoes on the ocean floor. Much of Puerto Rico is mountainous, but it has beautiful beaches, too.

Unit 5 • Reading Skills
Draw Conclusions

In this unit you will learn about the land, economy, and culture of the Midwest. Sometimes meanings and connections are not clear. Drawing conclusions is one way to better understand what you read. A conclusion is based on several pieces of information and explains what those facts mean.

Learn It

- As you read, ask yourself what the topic is about.
- Gather facts about the topic.
- Make a conclusion or a statement. It connects the facts you have gathered.
- Now read the paragraph below. Draw conclusions as you read.

Topic
Iowa grows much of the nation's corn.

Facts
Corn is fed to farm animals.

Facts
Corn is used in many everyday items.

Farmers in Iowa grow more than a million bushels of corn each year. Iowa leads the nation in corn production. Much of that corn is fed to farm animals such as hogs and cattle. Corn is also used to make crayons, paper, peanut butter, pet food, toothpaste, and margarine.

Try It

Copy the chart below. Then fill in the chart with your conclusions from the paragraph on page R10.

Text Clues	Conclusion

What did you use to help you draw conclusions?

Apply It

- Review the steps for drawing conclusions in Learn It.
- Read the passage below. Then draw conclusions using the information from the passage.
- Name some occasions when drawing conclusions can help you study.

In the last 20 years, many American fast food restaurants have opened in China. China also buys many food products from the United States. One of these products is soybeans. The United States sells more than $1 billion in soybeans to China each year. Some soybeans are used to produce cooking oil. Others are made into soybean meal to feed poultry and beef cattle.

Unit 6 • Reading Skills
Cause and Effect

In this unit you will learn about the land, economy, and culture of the Southwest. Thinking about causes and effects will help you understand how and why the Southwest has changed over time.

A cause is an event that makes something happen. An effect is what happens. When one thing causes another thing to happen, they have a cause-and-effect relationship.

Learn It

- As you read, ask yourself what happened. This will help you find an effect.

- Ask yourself why something happened. This will help you find a cause.

- Look for the words *because*, *therefore*, *so*, and *as a result*. These clue words point to causes and effects.

- Now read the paragraphs below. Look for causes and effects as you read.

Cause
Much of the Southwest belonged to Spain.

Effect
Many cities have Spanish names.

In the early 1600s, much of the Southwest belonged to Spain. The Spanish made settlements, including the city of Santa Fe, built in 1610. Spanish priests came because they wanted to teach the Native Americans Christianity. Later the lands of the Southwest became part of Mexico.

As a result of years under Spanish and Mexican rule, many places still have Spanish names. Spanish and Mexican foods are popular. People from Mexico and other Spanish-speaking countries still move to this part of our country, and many people speak Spanish.

Try It

Copy the chart below. Then fill in the chart with causes and effects from the paragraph on page R12.

Cause	→	Effect
	→	
	→	
	→	

What questions helped you identify cause and effect?

Apply It

- Review the steps for understanding cause and effect in Learn It.
- Read the passage below. Then create a cause and effect chart using the information.

Early settlers of the Southwest came to farm or start ranches. After World War II, many people moved to the region to get jobs in the oil and technology industries. Today people also move there to retire to a warmer climate. Therefore, the Southwest is one of the fastest growing regions in the United States.

Make Generalizations

As you read you sometimes come across information about things that seem to have nothing in common. On a closer look, however, you may see similarities. You might be able to make a generalization. A generalization is a broad statement that shows how different facts, people, or events have something in common.

Learn It

- As you read, ask yourself what the topic is about.
- Gather text clues about the topic.
- Look for similarities in the clues.
- Now read the paragraph below. Make generalizations as you read.

Text Clue
Montana has mountains rich in copper and silver.

Text Clue
Colorado has mountains rich in gold.

Text Clue
Wyoming has mountains that produce coal, oil, and uranium.

More than two-thirds of Montana is mountains. The mountains are rich in mineral deposits, such as copper and silver. Colorado has mountains, too. When gold was discovered in Colorado's mountains, thousands of people rushed there. Wyoming is a mountainous state, as well. Its mountains produce coal, oil, and uranium.

Try It

Copy the chart below. Then fill in the chart with your conclusions from the paragraph on page R14.

Text Clues	What You Know	Inferences

What steps did you take to make your generalization?

Apply It

- Review the steps for Make Generalizations in Learn It.
- Read the passage below. Then make generalizations using the information from the passage.
- Name some occasions when making generalizations may help you study.

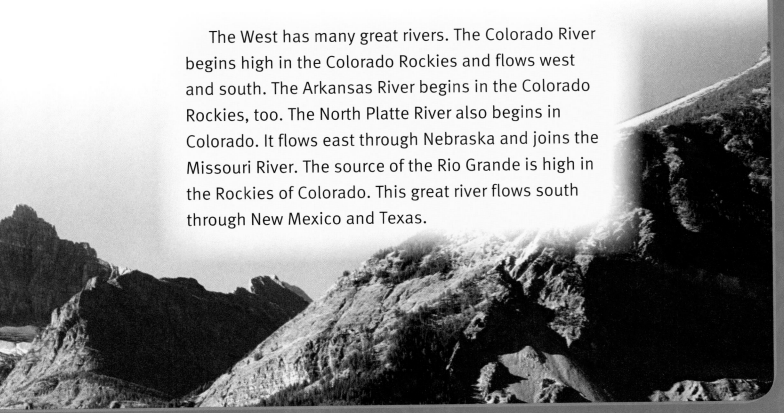

The West has many great rivers. The Colorado River begins high in the Colorado Rockies and flows west and south. The Arkansas River begins in the Colorado Rockies, too. The North Platte River also begins in Colorado. It flows east through Nebraska and joins the Missouri River. The source of the Rio Grande is high in the Rockies of Colorado. This great river flows south through New Mexico and Texas.

Geography Handbook

Geography and You

Geography is the study of our Earth and the people who live here. Most people think of geography as learning about cities, states, and countries, but geography is more than that. Geography includes learning about land, such as plains and mountains. Geography also helps us learn how to use land and water wisely.

Did you know that people are part of geography? Geography includes the study of how people adapt to live in a new place. How people move around, how they move goods, and how ideas travel from place to place are also parts of geography.

In fact, geography includes so many things that geographers have divided this information into six elements, or ideas, so you can better understand them.

Six Essential Elements

The World in Spatial Terms: Where is a place located, and what land or water features does this place have?

Places and Regions: What is special about a place, and what makes it different from other places?

Physical Systems: What has shaped the land and climate of a place, and how does this affect the plants, animals, and people there?

Human Systems: How do people, ideas, and goods move from place to place?

Environment and Society: How have people changed the land and water of a place, and how have the land and water affected the people of a place?

Uses of Geography: How does geography influence events in the past, present, and the future?

Five Themes of Geography

You have read about the six elements of geography. The five themes of geography are another way of dividing the ideas of geography. The themes, or topics, are **location**, **place**, **region**, **movement**, and **human interaction**. Using these five themes is another way to understand events you read about in this book.

1. Location

Washington, D. C.

In geography, *location* means an exact spot on the planet. A location is usually a street name and number. You write a location when you address a letter.

2. Place

Seattle, Washington

A *place* is described by its physical features, such as rivers, mountains, or valleys. You would also include the human features, such as cities, language, and traditions, in the description of a place.

3. Region

Florida Everglades National Park

A *region* is a larger area than a place or location. The people in a region are affected by landforms. Their region has typical jobs and customs. For example, the fertile soil of the Mississippi Lowlands helps farmers in the region grow crops.

4. Movement

Los Angeles, California

Throughout history, people have *moved* to find better land or a better life. Geographers study why these movements occurred. They also study how people's movements have changed a region.

5. Human Interaction

Pittsburgh, Pennsylvania

Geographers are interested in how people adapt to their environment. Geographers also study how people change their environment. This *interaction* between people and their environments determines how land is used for cities, farms, or parks.

Dictionary of Geographic Terms

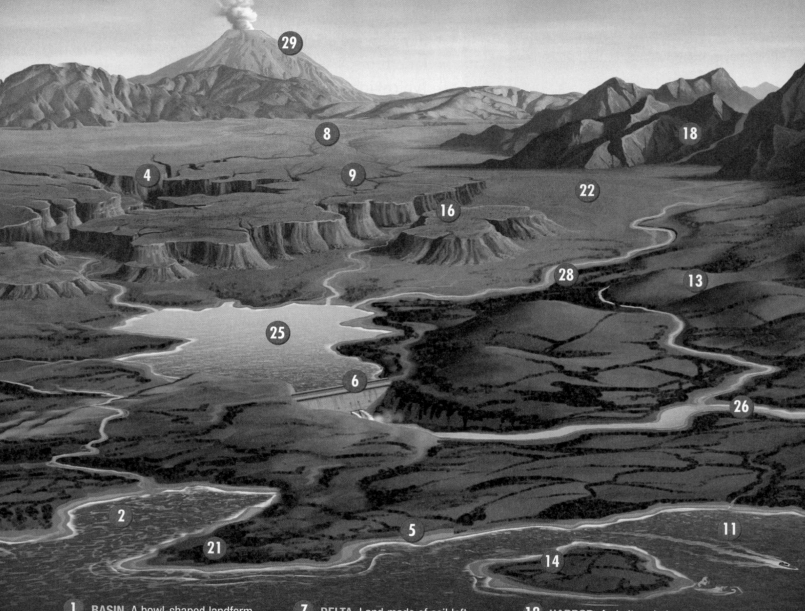

1 **BASIN** A bowl-shaped landform surrounded by higher land

2 **BAY** Part of an ocean or lake that extends deeply into the land

3 **CANAL** A channel built to carry water for irrigation or transportation

4 **CANYON** A deep, narrow valley with steep sides

5 **COAST** The land along an ocean

6 **DAM** A wall built across a river, creating a lake that stores water

7 **DELTA** Land made of soil left behind as a river drains into a larger body of water

8 **DESERT** A dry environment with few plants and animals

9 **FAULT** The border between two of the plates that make up Earth's crust

10 **GLACIER** A huge sheet of ice that moves slowly across the land

11 **GULF** Part of an ocean that extends into the land; larger than a bay

12 **HARBOR** A sheltered place along a coast where boats dock safely

13 **HILL** A rounded, raised landform; not as high as a mountain

14 **ISLAND** A body of land completely surrounded by water

15 **LAKE** A body of water completely surrounded by land

16 **MESA** A hill with a flat top; smaller than a plateau

17	**MOUNTAIN** A high landform with steep sides; higher than a hill	22	**PLAIN** A large area of nearly flat land	27	**SOURCE** The starting point of a river
18	**MOUNTAIN PASS** A narrow gap through a mountain range	23	**PLATEAU** A high, flat area that rises steeply above the surrounding land	28	**VALLEY** An area of low land between hills or mountains
19	**MOUTH** The place where a river empties into a larger body of water	24	**PORT** A place where ships load and unload their goods	29	**VOLCANO** An opening in Earth's surface through which hot rock and ash are forced out
20	**OCEAN** A large body of salt water; oceans cover much of Earth's surface	25	**RESERVOIR** A natural or artificial lake used to store water	30	**WATERFALL** A flow of water falling vertically
21	**PENINSULA** A body of land nearly surrounded by water	26	**RIVER** A stream of water that flows across the land and empties into another body of water		

Reviewing Geography Skills

Read a Physical Map

Maps are drawings of places on Earth. Most maps use colors and symbols to show information. Physical maps show and label landforms, such as mountains and deserts, and water features, such as lakes and rivers. Map makers use shading and color to show different physical features, such as blue to show water or dark shading to show mountains.

Map Title Map titles tell you what information is on the map.

Inset Map An inset map is a small map set into the main map. It shows an area that is too large, too small, or too far away to be included on the main map. Inset maps usually use a different scale than the main map.

Map Key The map key, or legend, gives the meaning of the colors and symbols on a map.

Map Scale The map scale is a line that shows the relationship between distances on a map and distances on Earth. Here, the length of the line on the map represents 400 miles on Earth.

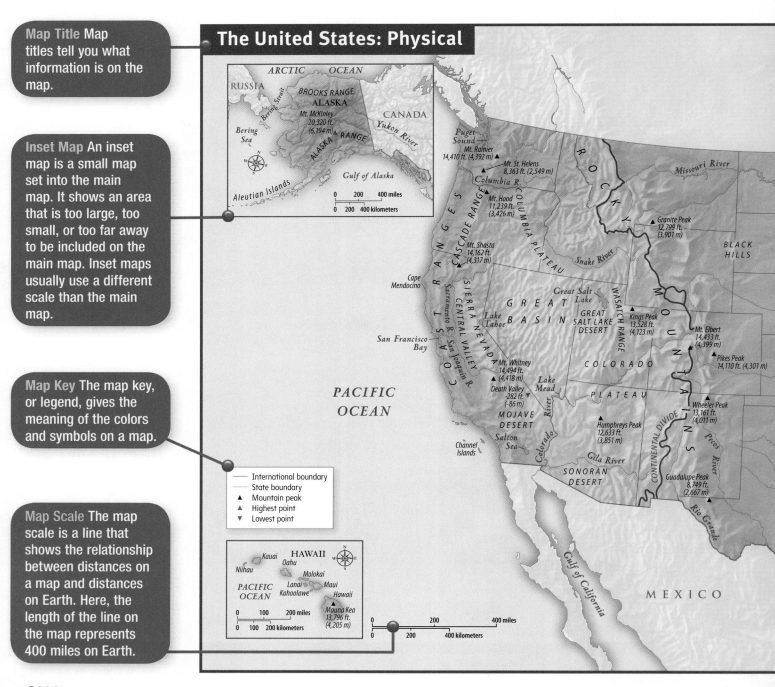

The United States: Physical

International boundary
State boundary
▲ Mountain peak
▲ Highest point
▼ Lowest point

Think About It About how far is it from Mt. Hood to Mt. Shasta in the Cascade Range?

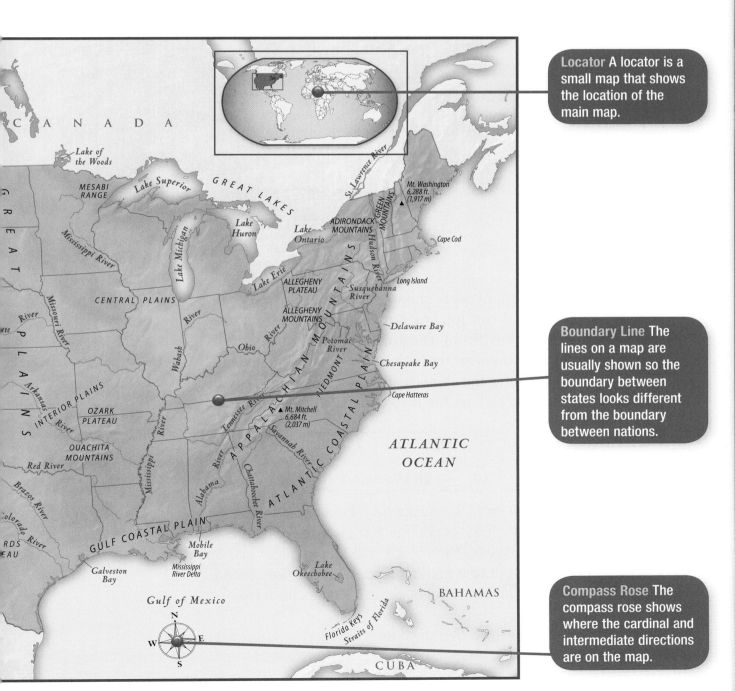

Locator A locator is a small map that shows the location of the main map.

Boundary Line The lines on a map are usually shown so the boundary between states looks different from the boundary between nations.

Compass Rose The compass rose shows where the cardinal and intermediate directions are on the map.

CANADA

Lake of the Woods

MESABI RANGE

Lake Superior

GREAT LAKES

Mississippi River

GREAT PLAINS

Lake Michigan

Lake Huron

Lake Ontario

St. Lawrence River

GREEN MOUNTAINS

Mt. Washington 6,288 ft. (1,917 m)

ADIRONDACK MOUNTAINS

Hudson River

Cape Cod

Lake Erie

ALLEGHENY PLATEAU

Susquehanna River

Long Island

CENTRAL PLAINS

Missouri River

Platte River

River

ALLEGHENY MOUNTAINS

Ohio River

Wabash

Potomac River

Delaware Bay

Chesapeake Bay

PIEDMONT

APPALACHIAN MOUNTAINS

Arkansas River

INTERIOR PLAINS

OZARK PLATEAU

Tennessee River

Mt. Mitchell 6,684 ft. (2,037 m)

ATLANTIC COASTAL PLAIN

Cape Hatteras

OUACHITA MOUNTAINS

Red River

Mississippi River

Savannah River

Alabama River

Chattahoochee River

ATLANTIC OCEAN

Brazos River

Colorado River

RDS EAU

GULF COASTAL PLAIN

Mobile Bay

Galveston Bay

Mississippi River Delta

Lake Okeechobee

BAHAMAS

Gulf of Mexico

N

W E

S

Florida Keys

Straits of Florida

CUBA

Read a Route Map

You know that many route maps show distances as shorter than they are on Earth. How can you find out how much shorter the distances are? Maps are drawn using map scales. A map scale shows a unit of measurement that stands for a real distance on Earth. Not all maps have the same scale. You can see on page GH9 that a distance of one inch on the map equals 50 miles on Earth.

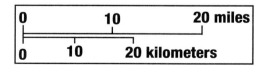

Look at the map. How far is Sandusky from Fremont? Place a slip of paper just below both cities. Make one mark where Fremont is and another where Sandusky is. Then place your slip of paper just under the map scale, with your first mark at zero. Where is the second mark? You can see that Sandusky is about 25 miles from Fremont.

Think About It How far is Mansfield from Oberlin?

Route Maps

Suppose you want to go somewhere you have never been before. How would you know which roads to take? You would use a route map. Route maps show the roads in a certain area. By reading a route map, you can figure out how to get from one place to another. Many route maps are also grid maps, like this one.

Grid Maps

A grid map has a special grid to help you locate things. Each box can be named with a number and a letter. For example, you might want to find Akron, Ohio, but you don't know where to look. You can see from the index that Akron is located in square B-3. Put one finger on the letter B along the side of the map. Put another finger on the number 3 at the top. Then move your fingers across and down the map until they meet. You have found B-3 on the grid, and now that you only have to search one square instead of the whole map, it's easy to find Akron.

Think About It Find Lima on the map. What grid box is it in?

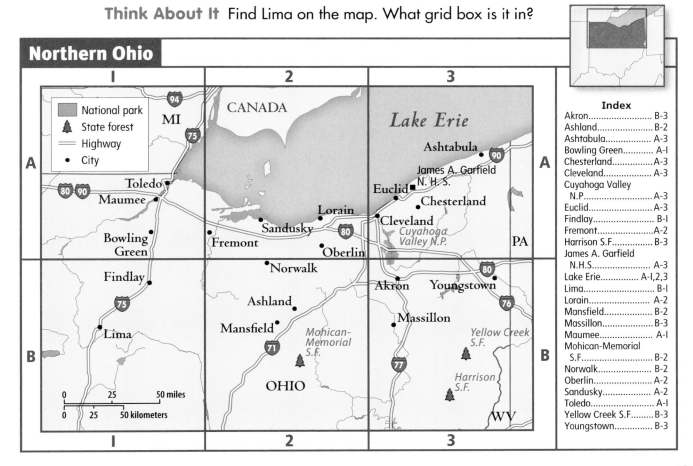

Northern Ohio

Index

Hemispheres

You can think of Earth as a sphere, like a ball or a globe. A hemisphere is half of a sphere. Geographers have divided Earth into the Northern Hemisphere and the Southern Hemisphere at the equator, an imaginary line that circles Earth halfway between the North Pole and the South Pole. Another important imaginary line is the prime meridian. It divides Earth from east to west. The area west of the prime meridian is called the Western Hemisphere, and the area east of the prime meridian is called the Eastern Hemisphere.

Think About It In which two hemispheres is North America?

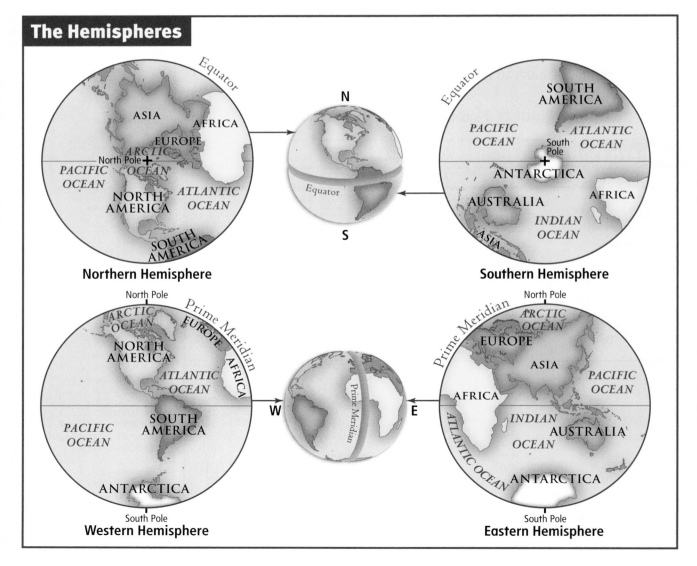

The Hemispheres

Northern Hemisphere

Southern Hemisphere

Western Hemisphere

Eastern Hemisphere

Latitude and Longitude

Earth can be divided into a grid of lines called latitude and longitude. Lines of latitude measure how far north or south a place is from the equator. Lines of longitude measure distance east or west from the prime meridian. Both the equator and the prime meridian represent 0 degrees. The symbol for degrees is °. Latitude lines measure the distance in degrees from the equator, and longitude lines measure the distance in degrees from the prime meridian. Look at the map. You can see that Los Angeles is located very near the longitude line labeled 120°W at the top of the map. That means that Los Angeles is about 120° west of the prime meridian.

Think About It Is Lagos north or south of the equator?

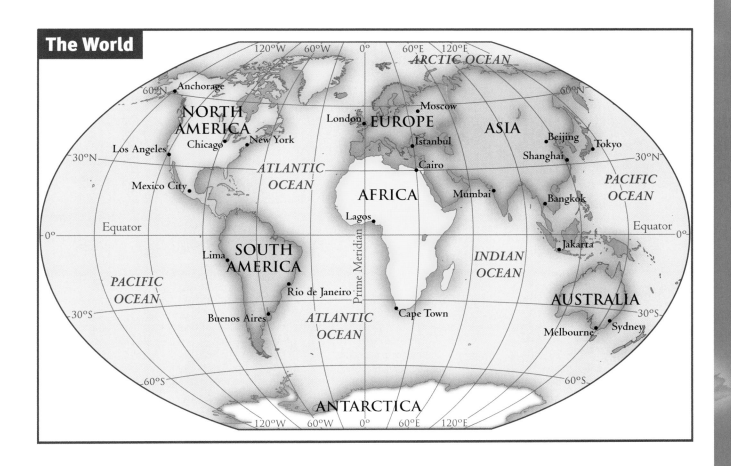

ARCTIC OCEAN

180°W · 70°N · 120°W

RUSSIA

CANADA

Arctic Circle

Nome · *Yukon R.* · Fairbanks

ALASKA

60°N

Anchorage

130°W

Juneau

W · N · E · S

0 · 200 · 400 miles
0 · 200 · 400 kilometers

170°W · 160°W · 150°W · 140°W

40°N · 130°W

Seattle · *River*
Olympia ★
WASHINGTON · Spokane
Columbia
Portland ★
Salem
Eugene
OREGON

Great Falls
Helena ★ · MONTANA · *Missouri River*
Billings

IDAHO
★ Boise
Snake River · Pocatello

WYOMING
Casper

Eureka
Redding
Great Salt Lake
Ogden
Salt Lake ★ · City · Provo
Cheyenne ★

Reno
Carson City ★
NEVADA
UTAH
Denver ★
COLORADO
Colorado Springs
Pueblo

Sacramento ★
San Francisco
Oakland
San Jose
Fresno
Colorado River

CALIFORNIA
Las Vegas

Bakersfield

PACIFIC
OCEAN

30°N

Santa Fe ★
Albuquerque

Los Angeles
Long Beach
ARIZONA
Phoenix ★
NEW MEXICO

San Diego
Tucson

Rio Grande · El Paso

0 · 200 · 400 miles
0 · 200 · 400 kilometers

130°W

160°W · HAWAII · 155°W
Kauai
Niihau · Oahu
Honolulu ★ · Molokai
PACIFIC · Lanai · Maui
OCEAN · Kahoolawe
20°N
Hilo
Hawaii

0 · 100 · 200 miles
0 · 100 · 200 kilometers

——	International boundary
——	State boundary
✪	National capital
★	State capital
•	Other city

MEXICO

Gulf of California

Tropic of Cancer

20°N

120°W · 110°W

CANADA

NORTH DAKOTA
Grand Forks
Fargo
Bismarck

SOUTH DAKOTA
Pierre
Sioux Falls

NEBRASKA
Platte River
Omaha
Lincoln

KANSAS
Topeka
Kansas City
Wichita

OKLAHOMA
Oklahoma City
Tulsa
Arkansas River
Red River

TEXAS
Fort Worth
Dallas
Brazos River
Austin
Colorado River
Houston
San Antonio
Corpus Christi
Laredo

MINNESOTA
Duluth
St. Paul
Minneapolis

IOWA
Cedar Rapids
Des Moines
Davenport

MISSOURI
Kansas City
Jefferson City
St. Louis

ARKANSAS
Fort Smith
Little Rock
Mississippi River

LOUISIANA
Shreveport
Baton Rouge
New Orleans

Lake Superior
Marquette
MICHIGAN
Lake Huron
Lake Michigan

WISCONSIN
Green Bay
Milwaukee
Madison
Chicago
Gary

ILLINOIS
Springfield
Indianapolis
INDIANA
Grand Rapids
Lansing

Detroit
Toledo
Cleveland
OHIO
Columbus
Cincinnati
Evansville
Ohio River
Louisville
Frankfort

KENTUCKY

TENNESSEE
Nashville
Tennessee River
Knoxville
Memphis

MISSISSIPPI
Jackson
Biloxi
Mobile

ALABAMA
Birmingham
Montgomery

GEORGIA
Atlanta
Columbus
Savannah

Lake Ontario
Lake Erie

NEW HAMPSHIRE
VERMONT
MAINE
Augusta
Portland
Montpelier
Concord

NEW YORK
Albany
Buffalo
Boston
MASSACHUSETTS
Hartford
Providence
RHODE ISLAND
CONNECTICUT

PENNSYLVANIA
Harrisburg
Newark
New York
Trenton
NEW JERSEY
Pittsburgh
Philadelphia
Baltimore
Dover
DELAWARE

Washington, D.C.
WEST VIRGINIA
Charleston
Annapolis
MARYLAND

Richmond
Norfolk
VIRGINIA

NORTH CAROLINA
Raleigh
Charlotte

SOUTH CAROLINA
Columbia
Charleston

ATLANTIC OCEAN

Tallahassee
Jacksonville

FLORIDA
Orlando
Tampa
Lake Okeechobee
Miami

Gulf of Mexico

BAHAMAS

CUBA

N
W E
S

70°W
50°N
40°N
30°N
100°W
90°W
80°W

GH13

Inset: Alaska
ARCTIC OCEAN
RUSSIA
BROOKS RANGE
ALASKA
Mt. McKinley
20,320 ft.
(6,194 m)
ALASKA RANGE
CANADA
Yukon River
Bering Strait
Bering Sea
Gulf of Alaska
Aleutian Islands

0 200 400 miles
0 200 400 kilometers

Main Map
Puget Sound
Mt. Rainier 14,410 ft. (4,392 m)
Mt. St. Helens 8,363 ft. (2,549 m)
Columbia R.
CASCADE RANGE
Mt. Hood 11,239 ft. (3,426 m)
COLUMBIA PLATEAU
ROCKY
Missouri River
Granite Peak 12,799 ft. (3,901 m)
BLACK HILLS
Mt. Shasta 14,162 ft. (4,317 m)
Snake River
Cape Mendocino
COAST RANGES
SIERRA NEVADA
CENTRAL VALLEY
Sacramento R.
San Joaquin R.
Great Salt Lake
GREAT BASIN
WASATCH RANGE
GREAT SALT LAKE DESERT
Kings Peak 13,528 ft. (4,123 m)
MOUNTAINS
Mt. Elbert 14,433 ft. (4,399 m)
Lake Tahoe
San Francisco Bay
Mt. Whitney 14,494 ft. (4,418 m)
Death Valley -282 ft. (-86 m)
Lake Mead
COLORADO
Pikes Peak 14,110 ft. (4,301 m)
PLATEAU
PACIFIC OCEAN
Colorado River
MOJAVE DESERT
Salton Sea
Channel Islands
Humphreys Peak 12,633 ft. (3,851 m)
Wheeler Peak 13,161 ft. (4,011 m)
CONTINENTAL DIVIDE
Pecos River
SONORAN DESERT
Gila River
Guadalupe Peak 8,749 ft. (2,667 m)
Rio Grande
Gulf of California
MEXICO

Legend
— International boundary
— State boundary
▲ Mountain peak
▲ Highest point
▼ Lowest point

Inset: Hawaii
Kauai
Niihau
Oahu
HAWAII
Molokai
Lanai Maui
Kahoolawe
Hawaii
PACIFIC OCEAN
Mauna Kea 13,796 ft. (4,205 m)

0 100 200 miles
0 100 200 kilometers

0 200 400 miles
0 200 400 kilometers

CANADA

Lake of the Woods

MESABI RANGE

Lake Superior

GREAT LAKES

St. Lawrence River

GREEN MOUNTAINS

Mt. Washington
6,288 ft.
(1,917 m) ▲

Lake Michigan

Lake Huron

ADIRONDACK MOUNTAINS

Hudson River

Cape Cod

Lake Ontario

G R E A T

Mississippi River

Lake Erie

ALLEGHENY PLATEAU

Susquehanna River

Long Island

CENTRAL PLAINS

River

ALLEGHENY MOUNTAINS

Delaware Bay

Platte River

Missouri River

Wabash River

River

Ohio

APPALACHIAN MOUNTAINS

Potomac River

Chesapeake Bay

P L A I N S

INTERIOR PLAINS

Arkansas River

OZARK PLATEAU

Mississippi River

Tennessee River

PIEDMONT

Cape Hatteras

▲ Mt. Mitchell
6,684 ft.
(2,037 m)

OUACHITA MOUNTAINS

River

Savannah River

ATLANTIC OCEAN

Red River

Brazos River

Alabama River

Chattahoochee River

ATLANTIC COASTAL PLAIN

Colorado River

EDWARDS PLATEAU

GULF COASTAL PLAIN

Mobile Bay

Lake Okeechobee

Galveston Bay

Mississippi River Delta

Gulf of Mexico

BAHAMAS

Florida Keys

Straits of Florida

N
W   E
S

CUBA

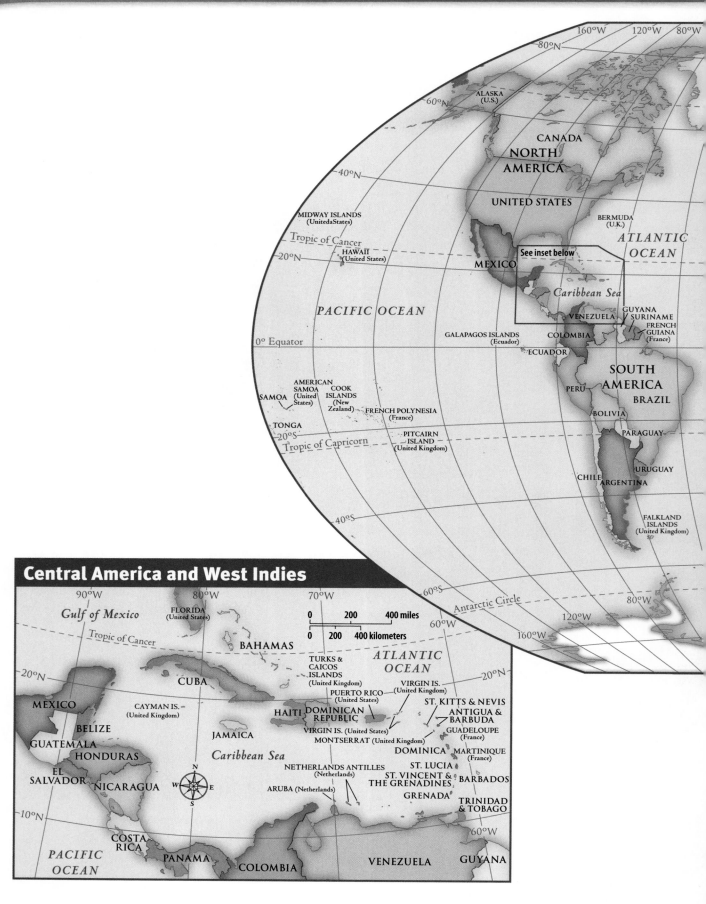

160°W   120°W   80°W

80°N

60°N

ALASKA
(U.S.)

CANADA

NORTH
AMERICA

40°N

UNITED STATES

BERMUDA
(U.K.)

ATLANTIC
OCEAN

MIDWAY ISLANDS
(UnitedaStates)

Tropic of Cancer

20°N

HAWAII
(United States)

MEXICO

See inset below

Caribbean Sea

GUYANA
SURINAME

PACIFIC OCEAN

VENEZUELA

FRENCH
GUIANA
(France)

GALAPAGOS ISLANDS
(Ecuador)

COLOMBIA

0° Equator

ECUADOR

SOUTH
AMERICA

AMERICAN
SAMOA
(United
States)

COOK
ISLANDS
(New
Zealand)

PERU

BRAZIL

SAMOA

FRENCH POLYNESIA
(France)

BOLIVIA

TONGA

20°S

PITCAIRN
ISLAND
(United Kingdom)

PARAGUAY

Tropic of Capricorn

CHILE

URUGUAY

ARGENTINA

40°S

FALKLAND
ISLANDS
(United Kingdom)

60°S

Antarctic Circle

60°W

80°W

120°W

160°W

Central America and West Indies

90°W   80°W   70°W

Gulf of Mexico

FLORIDA
(United States)

0   200   400 miles

0   200   400 kilometers

Tropic of Cancer

BAHAMAS

ATLANTIC
OCEAN

20°N

CUBA

TURKS &
CAICOS
ISLANDS
(United Kingdom)

VIRGIN IS.
(United Kingdom)

20°N

MEXICO

CAYMAN IS.
(United Kingdom)

PUERTO RICO
(United States)

ST. KITTS & NEVIS

HAITI DOMINICAN
REPUBLIC

ANTIGUA &
BARBUDA

BELIZE

JAMAICA

VIRGIN IS. (United States)

GUADELOUPE
(France)

GUATEMALA

MONTSERRAT (United Kingdom)

DOMINICA

MARTINIQUE
(France)

HONDURAS

Caribbean Sea

EL
SALVADOR

NICARAGUA

NETHERLANDS ANTILLES
(Netherlands)

ST. LUCIA

ST. VINCENT &
THE GRENADINES

BARBADOS

N
W   E
S

ARUBA (Netherlands)

GRENADA

TRINIDAD
& TOBAGO

10°N

60°W

COSTA
RICA

PACIFIC
OCEAN

PANAMA

COLOMBIA

VENEZUELA

GUYANA

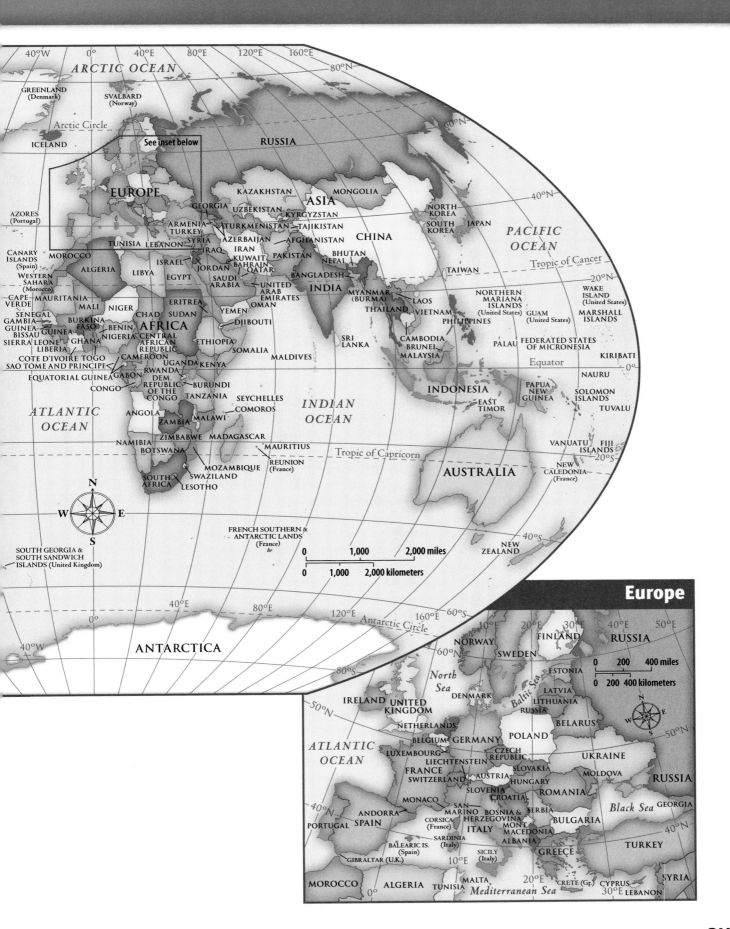

40°W 0° 40°E 80°E 120°E 160°E

ARCTIC OCEAN

80°N

GREENLAND
(Denmark)

SVALBARD
(Norway)

Arctic Circle

ICELAND

60°N

RUSSIA

See inset below

EUROPE

40°N

ASIA

KAZAKHSTAN

MONGOLIA

AZORES
(Portugal)

GEORGIA

UZBEKISTAN

KYRGYZSTAN

ARMENIA
TURKEY

TURKMENISTAN

TAJIKISTAN

NORTH
KOREA

SOUTH
KOREA

JAPAN

PACIFIC
OCEAN

CANARY
ISLANDS
(Spain)

MOROCCO

TUNISIA

LEBANON

SYRIA

AZERBAIJAN

AFGHANISTAN

CHINA

ALGERIA

ISRAEL

IRAQ

IRAN

PAKISTAN

BHUTAN

TAIWAN

Tropic of Cancer

WESTERN
SAHARA
(Morocco)

LIBYA

JORDAN

KUWAIT

BAHRAIN

QATAR

NEPAL

20°N

EGYPT

SAUDI
ARABIA

BANGLADESH

WAKE
ISLAND
(United States)

CAPE
VERDE

MAURITANIA

MALI

NIGER

ERITREA

YEMEN

UNITED
ARAB
EMIRATES

OMAN

INDIA

MYANMAR
(BURMA)

LAOS

NORTHERN
MARIANA
ISLANDS
(United States)

GUAM
(United States)

MARSHALL
ISLANDS

SENEGAL
GAMBIA
GUINEA-
BISSAU
SIERRA LEONE
LIBERIA

BURKINA
FASO

GUINEA

GHANA

BENIN

NIGERIA

CHAD

CENTRAL
AFRICAN
REPUBLIC

SUDAN

AFRICA

DJIBOUTI

ETHIOPIA

SOMALIA

THAILAND

VIETNAM

CAMBODIA

SRI
LANKA

MALDIVES

PHILIPPINES

BRUNEI

PALAU

FEDERATED STATES
OF MICRONESIA

KIRIBATI

COTE D'IVOIRE TOGO
SAO TOME AND PRINCIPE

CAMEROON

UGANDA

KENYA

MALAYSIA

EQUATORIAL GUINEA

GABON

RWANDA

DEM.
REPUBLIC
OF THE
CONGO

BURUNDI

NAURU

Equator

0°

CONGO

TANZANIA

SEYCHELLES

INDONESIA

PAPUA
NEW
GUINEA

SOLOMON
ISLANDS

COMOROS

INDIAN
OCEAN

EAST
TIMOR

TUVALU

ATLANTIC
OCEAN

ANGOLA

ZAMBIA

MALAWI

ZIMBABWE

MADAGASCAR

NAMIBIA

BOTSWANA

MAURITIUS

Tropic of Capricorn

VANUATU

FIJI
ISLANDS

20°S

SOUTH
AFRICA

MOZAMBIQUE

SWAZILAND

LESOTHO

REUNION
(France)

AUSTRALIA

NEW
CALEDONIA
(France)

N
W   E
S

SOUTH GEORGIA &
SOUTH SANDWICH
ISLANDS (United Kingdom)

FRENCH SOUTHERN &
ANTARCTIC LANDS
(France)

0   1,000   2,000 miles

0   1,000   2,000 kilometers

40°S

NEW
ZEALAND

40°E   80°E   120°E   160°E   60°S

Antarctic Circle

0°

ANTARCTICA

40°W   80°S

60°N   10°E   20°E   30°E   40°E   50°E

NORWAY

FINLAND

RUSSIA

SWEDEN

0   200   400 miles

0   200   400 kilometers

North
Sea

ESTONIA

Baltic Sea

LATVIA

LITHUANIA

RUSSIA

IRELAND

UNITED
KINGDOM

DENMARK

50°N

BELARUS

50°N

N

NETHERLANDS

POLAND

W   E
S

ATLANTIC
OCEAN

BELGIUM

GERMANY

UKRAINE

LUXEMBOURG

CZECH
REPUBLIC

LIECHTENSTEIN

SLOVAKIA

MOLDOVA

RUSSIA

FRANCE

AUSTRIA

HUNGARY

ROMANIA

SWITZERLAND

SLOVENIA

CROATIA

40°N

MONACO

SAN
MARINO

BOSNIA &
HERZEGOVINA

SERBIA

Black Sea

GEORGIA

ANDORRA

CORSICA
(France)

MONT.

BULGARIA

PORTUGAL

SPAIN

ITALY

MACEDONIA

ALBANIA

40°N

BALEARIC IS.
(Spain)

SARDINIA
(Italy)

SICILY
(Italy)

GREECE

TURKEY

GIBRALTAR (U.K.)

10°E

MALTA

CRETE (Gr.)

CYPRUS

SYRIA

MOROCCO

ALGERIA

0°

TUNISIA

20°E

Mediterranean Sea

30°E

LEBANON

NORTH AMERICA: POLITICAL/PHYSICAL

EUROPE

ASIA

ARCTIC OCEAN

Arctic Circle

140°E
150°E
160°E
170°E
180°
170°W
160°W

Chukchi Sea

Bering Sea

Bering Strait

Point Barrow

NORTH SLOPE

BROOKS RANGE

Yukon R.

ALASKA

SEWARD PENINSULA

Mt. McKinley
20,320 ft.
(6,194 m)

ALASKA RANGE

KENAI PENINSULA

Kodiak Island

Gulf of Alaska

Mt. Logan
19,551 ft.
(5,959 m)

YUKON PLATEAU

MACKENZIE MTS.

Mackenzie R.

ALEXANDER ARCHIPELAGO

Queen Charlotte Islands

Vancouver Island

FRASER PLATEAU

COLUMBIA MTS.

Peace R.

Slave R.

Athabasca R.

OLYMPIC PENINSULA

COAST MOUNTAINS

COLUMBIA PLATEAU

Snake R.

Great Salt Lake

Cape Mendocino

COAST RANGES

CASCADE RANGE

SIERRA NEVADA

GREAT BASIN

COLORADO PLATEAU

Mt. Whitney
14,494 ft.
(4,418 m)

Death Valley
-282 ft.
(-86 m)

Channel Islands

Grand Canyon

Colorado R.

SONORAN DESERT

BAJA CALIFORNIA

Gulf of California

Beaufort Sea

Banks Island

Melville Island

Victoria Island

Prince of Wales I.

Somerset I.

BOOTHIA PENINSULA

MELVILLE PEN.

Queen Elizabeth Islands

Ellesmere Island

Devon Island

Oodaaq Island

Lincoln Sea

HAYES PENINSULA

Greenland Sea

Gunnbjorn
12,139 ft.
(3,700 m)

ICELAND

Greenland

Baffin Bay

Baffin Island

Foxe Basin

Southampton Island

Hudson Strait

Davis Strait

Cape Farewell

Labrador Sea

Arctic Circle

CANADA

Great Bear Lake

Great Slave Lake

Lake Athabasca

Churchill R.

Saskatchewan R.

Lake Winnipeg

ROCKY MOUNTAINS

GREAT PLAINS

CANADIAN SHIELD

Hudson Bay

Belcher Islands

James Bay

Ungava Bay

Island of Newfoundland

AVALON PENINSULA

Cape Breton Island

GASPÉ PEN.

LAURENTIAN MTS.

Gulf of St. Lawrence

St. Lawrence R.

Prince Edward Island

Nova Scotia

Lake Superior

Lake Michigan

Lake Huron

Lake Ontario

Lake Erie

Ottawa

APPALACHIAN MOUNTAINS

Gulf of Maine

Bay of Fundy

Cape Cod

Long Island

UNITED STATES

Missouri River

Platte R.

Arkansas River

Red River

CENTRAL LOWLAND

OZARK PLATEAU

Mississippi R.

Ohio R.

HIGH PLAINS

Washington, D.C.

Chesapeake Bay

Cape Hatteras

ATLANTIC OCEAN

Bermuda (U.K.)

COASTAL PLAIN

Rio Grande

SIERRA MADRE OCCIDENTAL

SIERRA MADRE ORIENTAL

MEXICO

Gulf of Mexico

México City

Orizaba
18,855 ft.
(5,747 m)

YUCATÁN PENINSULA

Cozumel Island

GUATEMALA

Isthmus of Tehuantepec

Guatemala City

San Salvador

EL SALVADOR

BELIZE

Belmopan

HONDURAS

Tegucigalpa

Managua

NICARAGUA

Lake Nicaragua

COSTA RICA

San José

PANAMA

Panamá

Isthmus of Panama

BAHAMAS

Nassau

Havana

Florida Keys

CUBA

Cayman Islands (U.K.)

Kingston

JAMAICA

HAITI

Port-au-Prince

Hispaniola

DOMINICAN REPUBLIC

Santo Domingo

Puerto Rico (U.S.)

Virgin Islands

Guadeloupe

Martinique

WEST INDIES

Caribbean Sea

TRINIDAD & TOBAGO

Port-of-Spain

PACIFIC OCEAN

Tropic of Cancer

CENTRAL AMERICA

SOUTH AMERICA

Equator

Legend	
—	International boundary
✪	National capital
▲	Mountain peak

0   300   600 miles
0   300   600 kilometers

N
W   E
S

GH18

Glossary

This glossary will help you to pronounce and understand the meanings of the vocabulary in this book. The page number at the end of the definition tells you where the word first appears.

Pronunciation Key									
a	at	ē	me	ô	fork	ü	rule	th	thin
ā	ape	i	in	oi	oil	ů	pull	th	this
ä	far	ī	ice	ou	out	ûr	turn	zh	measure
âr	care	o	hot	u	up	hw	white	ə	about, taken, pencil,
e	end	ō	old	ū	use	ng	song		lemon, circus

A

adobe (ə dō'bē) A brick made of clay that is sometimes mixed with straw and then dried in the sun. (p. 247)

agribusiness (ag'ri biz nis) A large farm owned by a company. (p. 210)

agriculture (ag'ri kul chər) The science and business of growing crops and raising animals. (p. 82)

Allies (al'īz) The countries that fought against the Axis Powers in World War II —Great Britain, France, United States, and the Soviet Union among many others. (p. 55)

aquifer (ak'wə fər) A layer of rock or gravel that traps water underground and supplies wells and springs. (p. 237)

article (är'ti kəl) A story in a newspaper describing an important event that has taken place recently.

artifact (är'tə fakt) An object such as a tool or weapon made by people in the past. (p. 9)

B

assembly line (ə sem'blē līn) A line of workers and machines used for putting together a product step by step in a factory. (p. 212)

Axis (ak səs) The countries that fought against the Allied Powers in World War II —Germany, Italy, and Japan among many others. (p. 55)

B

bar graph (bär graf) A graph that can be used to show changes over time or changes among different types of information. (p. 205)

basin (bā'sin) A low landform, shaped like a bowl and surrounded by higher land. (p. 74)

bay (bā) A body of water surrounded by land on three sides. (p. 136)

bison (bis ən) A large, shaggy animal with short horns and a hump on its back. (p. 281)

blizzard (bliz'ərd) A heavy snowstorm with very strong winds.

bluegrass (blü'gras) A kind of folk music played on fiddles, banjos, and guitars popular in the Appalachian Mountains. (p. 188)

butte (būt) A flat-topped mountain or hill that stands alone in an area of flat land. (p. 233)

byline (bī'līn) The part of a newspaper article that tells the reader who wrote the story.

canal (kə nal') A human-made waterway built for boats and ships to travel through, and for carrying water to places that need it. (p. 36)

canyon (kan'yən) A deep valley with very high, steep sides. (p. 234)

capital resources (kap'i təl rē'sôr sez) The tools, machines, and factories businesses use to produce goods. (p. 101)

checks and balances (cheks and bal'an səz) A system in which the power of each branch of government is balanced by the powers of the other branches. (p. 108)

circle graph (sûr'kəl graf) A graph in the shape of a circle that shows how the different parts of something fit into a whole; also called a pie graph. (p. 173)

citizen (sit'ə zən) A person who was born in a country or who has earned the right to become a member of a country by law. (p. 115)

civil rights (siv'əl rīts) The rights of every citizen to be treated equally under the law. (p. 58)

Civil War (siv'əl wôr) The war between the Union states of the North and the Confederate states of the South, 1861–1865. (p. 41)

climate (klī'mət) The pattern of weather of a certain place over many years. (p. 85)

colony (kol'ə nē) A place that is ruled by another country. (p. 19)

communism (kom'yə niz əm) A system in which business, property, and goods are owned by the government. (p. 57)

conservationist (kon sər vā'shə nist) A person who supports the wise use and protection of natural resources. (p. 279)

constitution (kon sti tu'shən) A plan of government. (p. 108)

consumer (kən sü'mər) A person who buys goods and uses services. (p. 96)

county (koun'tē) One of the sections into which a state or country is divided. (p. 110)

credit (kred'it) A way to purchase something, in which a person borrows money that must be repaid, usually with interest. (p. 102)

culture (kul'chər) The arts, beliefs, and customs that make up a way of life for a group of people. (p. 151)

Declaration of Independence (dek lə rā'shən uv in də pen'dəns) A document written in 1776 by colonists telling the world why the colonies wanted independence. (p. 27)

degree (di grē') A unit for measuring distance on Earth's surface. (p. 112)

demand (di mand') The amount of goods and services that consumers are willing and able to buy at certain prices during a given time. (p. 95)

democracy (di mok'rə sē) A system of government in which people elect their leaders. (p. 115)

descendant (di send'ənt) A person who is related to a particular person or group of people who lived long ago. (p. 215)

dialect (dī'ə lekt) A form of a language spoken in a certain place by a certain group of people. (p. 185)

dictator (dik tā'tər) A person who rules a country without sharing power or consulting anyone else. (p. 55)

discrimination (di skrim' ə nā shən) An unfair difference in the way people are treated. (p. 58)

diverse (dī vûrs') Great difference; variety. (p. 153)

drought (drout) A long period of time when there is very little rain or no rain at all. (p. 236)

E

earthquake (ûrth'kwāk) A shaking of the earth. (p. 266)

economy (i kon'ə mē) The way a country or other place uses or produces natural resources, goods, and services. (p. 82)

editorial (ed' i tôr'ē əl) A newspaper article that offers a personal opinion about a topic.

elevation (el ə vā'shən) The height of land above sea level. (p. 77)

Emancipation Proclamation (i man sə pā'shən prok lə mā'shən) An announcement by President Lincoln in 1863 that all enslaved people living in Confederate states were free. (p. 43)

erosion (i rō'zhən) A wearing away of Earth's surface. (p. 72)

executive branch (eg zek'yə tiv branch) The branch of government that signs bills into laws. (p. 108)

expedition (ek spi dish'ən) A journey of exploration. (p. 34)

F

fall line (fôl līn) A line joining the waterfalls on numerous rivers where an upland meets a lowland. (p. 138)

federal (fed'ər əl) A system of government that shares power between state, local, and national governments. (p. 115)

fertile (fûr'təl) Land that is able to produce crops and plants easily and plentifully. (p. 200)

frontier (frun tîr') The far edge of a settled area. (p. 38)

fuel (fū'əl) Something used to produce energy. (p. 136)

G

geyser (gī'zər) A hot, underground spring from which steam and hot water shoot into the air. (p. 267)

glacier (glā'shər) A large mass of ice that moves slowly. (p. 135)

graph (graf) A diagram that represents information. (pp. 105, 173)

grid (grid) A set of squares formed by crisscrossing lines that can help you determine locations, such as on a map or globe. (p. 112)

H

headline (hed'līn) Words printed at the top of an article or story which tell the reader what the story is about.

historian (his tôr'ē ən) A person who studies the past.

human resources (hyü mən rē'sôr sez) All the people employed at a business or organization. (p. 101)

hunter-gatherer (hun'tər gath'ər ər) A person who found food by both hunting animals and gathering plants, fruit, and nuts. (p. 11)

hurricane (hûr'i kān) A storm with very strong winds and heavy rain. (p. 90)

I

immigrant (im'i grənt) A person who comes to a new country to live. (p. 46)

independent (in di pen'dənt) Free from the control of others. (p. 30)

industry (in'də strē) All the businesses that make one kind of product or provide one kind of service. (p. 145)

interdependent (in'tər di pen'dənt) Relying on one another to meet needs and wants. (p. 82)

interest (in'tər ist) Money that is paid for the use of borrowed or deposited money. (p. 102)

interstate highway (in'tər stāt hī'wā) A road with at least two lanes of traffic in each direction that connects two or more states. (p. 270)

invention (in ven'shən) A product that is made for the first time. (p. 47)

investor (in vest'ər) A person or company that uses money to buy something that will make more money. (p. 95)

iron (ī'ərn) A hard metal mainly used to make steel. (p. 208)

irrigation (ir i gā'shən) The use of ditches or pipes to bring water to dry land. (p. 242)

J

jazz (jaz) The form of popular music that grew out of African American culture in the 1920s. (p. 188)

judicial branch (jü dish'əl branch) The branch of government that interprets the laws. (p. 108)

jury (jür'ē) A group of citizens in a court of law who decide if someone accused of a crime is innocent or guilty. (p. 121)

justice (ju'stis) Fair treatment. (p. 124)

K

kerosene (kar'ə sēn) A fuel made from petroleum. (p. 241)

L

lake effect (lāk i fekt') The effect water has in changing the weather nearby. (p. 88)

large-scale map (lärj skāl map) A map that shows many details in a small area. (p. 141)

latitude (lat'i tüd) A measure of the distance north or south of the equator on Earth. (p. 112)

legislative branch (lej'is lā tiv branch) The branch of government that makes laws. (p. 108)

levee (le'vē) A wall of earth built along a river to keep the river from overflowing onto land. (p. 172)

line graph (līn graf) A graph that shows patterns and amounts of change over time. (pp. 105, 205)

longitude (lon'ji tüd) A measure of distance east or west of the prime meridian on Earth. (p. 112)

Louisiana Purchase (lü ē zē an'ə pûr'chəs) The territory purchased by the United States from France in 1803. (p. 34)

M

magma (mag'ə) Melted rock. (p. 266)

map scale (map scāl) The measurement a map uses to represent real distance on Earth. (p. 141)

mass production (mas prə duk'shən) The process of making large numbers of one product quickly. (p. 212)

megalopolis (meg ə lop'ə lis) A large urban area formed by several cities. (p. 149)

meridian (mə rid'ē ən) A line of longitude; see longitude. (p. 112)

mesa (mā'sə) A hill or mountain with a flat top and steep sides; a high plateau (p. 233)

migration (mī grā'shən) A large movement of people or animals from one place to another (p. 217)

mineral (min'ər əl) A nonrenewable resource found in nature that is not an animal or plant. (p. 71)

mission (mish'ən) A Spanish settlement in the Americas where priests talked about the Christian religion. (p. 18)

mouth (mouth') The place where a river empties into a larger body of water. (p. 167)

municipal (mū nis'ə pəl) Having to do with local or city government. (p. 110)

N

Natural resources (nach'ər əl rē'sôr sez) Materials found in nature that people use. (p. 101)

newspaper (nüz'pā pər) A paper that is usually printed daily or weekly and contains news, opinions, and advertising.

nonrenewable resource (non ri nü'ə bəl rē'sôrs) A thing found in nature that cannot be replaced such as coal. (p. 177)

Northwest Passage (nôrth' west' pas'ij) A water route from Europe to Asia through North America. (p. 19)

O

official document (ə fish'əl dok'yə mənt) A document that contains information that has been agreed upon by one or more people or institutions.

open-pit mining (ō'pən pit mī'ning) A method of removing ore deposits close to the surface of the ground using power shovels. (p. 208)

opportunity cost (opər tū'ni tē kôst) The alternatives that are given up because a particular choice was made. (p. 97)

ore (ôr) A mineral or rock that is mined for the metal or other substance it contains. (p. 208)

P

parallel (par'ə lel) A line of latitude. (p. 112)

patriotism (pā'trē ə tiz'əm) A love for and loyal support of one's country. (p. 123)

peninsula (pə nin'sə lə) Land that has water on three sides. (p. 168)

petroleum (pə trō'lē əm) A fuel, commonly called oil, that forms underground from dead plants. (p. 176)

pioneer (pī ə nîr') A person who leads the way or one who settles a new part of the country. (p. 217)

plateau (pla tō') An area of flat land, higher than the surrounding country. (p. 74)

population density (pop ū lā'shən den'sə tē) A measurement of how many people live in a particular area; a type of map that shows the same. (p. 238)

population distribution (pop ū lā'shən dis trə bū'shən) A measurement of where in an area people live; a type of map that shows the same. (p. 238)

powwow (pou'wou) A Native American festival. (p. 252)

prairie (prâr'ē) Flat or rolling land covered with grass. (p. 202)

precipitation (pri sip i tā'shən) The moisture that falls to the ground in the form of rain, sleet, hail, or snow. (p. 86)

prehistory (prē his'tōr ē) The time before written records. (p. 9)

primary source (prī'mer ē sôrs) An artifact, photograph, or eyewitness account of an event in the past.

prime meridian (prīm mə rid'ē ən) The line of longitude, marked 0°, from which other meridians are numbered. (p. 112)

producer (prə dū'sər) A person or company that makes or creates something. (p. 100)

profit (prof'it) The money a business earns after it pays for tools, salaries, and other costs. (p. 94)

pueblo (pweb' lō) Native American town or village with adobe and stone houses; any Native American group or people who live or whose ancestors lived in adobe or stone houses usually in the Southwest United States. (p. 247)

R

rain shadow (rān shad'ō) The side of the mountain that is usually dry because precipitation falls on the other side. (p. 87)

Reconstruction (rē kən struk'shən) The period after the Civil War in which Congress passed laws designed to rebuild the country and bring the Southern states back into the Union. (p. 44)

refinery (ri fī'nə rē) A factory which turns crude oil into useful products such as heating oil, gasoline, plastics, and paint. (p. 176)

region (rē'jen) An area, or group of states, with common features that set it apart from other areas. (p. 79)

renewable resource (ri nü' ə bəl rē'sôrs) A natural resource that can be replaced, such as trees or water. (p. 176)

reservation (rez ûr vā'shən) Land set aside by the government as settlements for Native Americans. (p. 119)

resource (rē' sôrs') A person, thing, or material that can be used for help or support. (p. 10)

revolution (rev ə lü'shən) The overthrow of a government. (p. 25)

road map (rōd map) A map that shows roads. (p. 270)

rodeo (rōd ē ō) A rodeo is a show that has contests in horseback riding, roping, and other similar skills. (p. 285)

rule of law (rool əv lô) The belief that a country's laws apply to all of its people equally. (p. 124)

S

sea level (sē lev'əl) The level of the surface of the sea. (p. 77)

secondary source (sek'ən der e sôrs) An account of an event from a person who did not see or experience it.

segregation (seg ri gā'shən) The practice of keeping racial groups separate. (p. 186)

service (sûr'vis) Something that is done to help another person. (p. 146)

silicon (sil i kän) A material used in the manufacture of computer chips. (p. 244)

small-scale map (smôl skāl map) A map that shows few details of a large area. (p. 141)

solar energy (sō'lər en'ər jē) Energy that comes from the sun. (p. 244)

source (sôrs) The starting point of a river. (p. 167)

sovereign (sov'ər in) A nation or group of people not controlled by others; independent. (p. 119)

suburban (sə bûr'ben) Describes a community near a city. (p. 149)

suffrage (suf'rij) The right to vote. (p. 51)

supply (sə plī) The amount of an item available at certain prices during a given time. (p. 95)

T

tax (taks) Money people and businesses must pay to the government so that it can provide public services. (p. 25)

technology (tek nol'ə jē) The use of skills, tools, and machines to meet people's needs; new method of doing something. (p. 13)

telecommunications (tel'i kə mū ni kā' shənz) The technology that allows people to send messages and images long distances quickly. (p. 276)

territory (ter'i tôr'ē) Land owned by a country either within or outside the country's borders. (p. 33)

terrorism (ter'ə riz əm) The use of violence and threats to acheive a political goal. (p. 60)

timberline (tim'bər līn) A tree line. (p. 268)

tornado (tôr nā'dō) A powerful wind storm with a funnel-shaped cloud that moves quickly over land. (p. 90)

tourist (tur'ist) A person who is traveling for pleasure. (p. 140)

tradition (trə dish'ən) A custom that is passed down from parents to their children. This includes festivals, songs, and dances. (p. 219)

tributary (trib'yə ter ē) A river or stream that flows into a larger river. (p. 73)

U

urban (ûr'bən) A city and its surrounding areas. (p. 148)

V

veto (vē'tō) The power of the executive branch to reject a bill passed by the legislature. (p. 109)

W

wetland (wet'land) A low flat area covered with water. (p. 167)

Index

This index lists many topics that appear in the book, along with the pages on which they are found. Page numbers after a *c* refer you to a chart or diagram, after a *g*, to a graph, after an *m*, to a map, after a *p*, to a photograph or picture, and after a *q*, to a quotation.

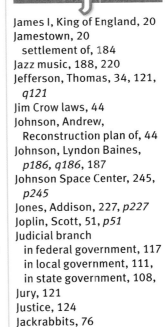

Index

Index

Credits

Illustration Credits: 132-133: Roger Stewart. 152-153: Roger Stewart. 158-159: Chuck Carter. 196: Robert Papp. 240: John Kurtz. 264: Inklink. 294-295: (b) Frank Ricco

Photo Credits: All Photographs are by Macmillan/McGraw-Hill (MMH) except as noted below.

Volume 2: iv-v: (bkgd) Dallas and John Heaton/Corbis. V: (br) Siede Preis/Getty Images. Viii: (bkgd) Robert J. Hurt Landscape Photography. Vi-vii: (bkgd) Michael Busselle/Digital Vision/Getty Images

COV (bl)Bettmann/CORBIS, (br)Tom Carter/PhotoEdit, (t)Imagemore/SuperStock; TTLPG Tom Carter/PhotoEdit; GH-GH1 (bg)Joseph Sohm; Visions of America/CORBIS; GH2 (t)Charles Smith/CORBIS, (b)Ken Straiton/CORBIS; GH3 (t)Iconotec/Alamy Images, (c)Mark Richards/PhotoEdit, (b)Gibson Stock Photography; RF (t)CORBIS, (c)The Granger Collection, New York, (b)Stockdisc/Getty Images; R6-R7 (b)Terry W. Eggers/CORBIS; R8-R9 (bg)Robert J. Hurt Landscape Photography; R10-R11 (b)Grant Heilman Photography; R13 (b)David Bacon/The Image Works, Inc.; R14-R15 (b)Lorenz Britt/Alamy Images; iv-v (bg)Sime s.a.s./eStock Photo/eStock Photo; vi (inset)Lake County (IL)Discovery Museum, Curt Teich Postcard Archives; vi-vii (b)Michael Busselle/Digital Vision/SuperStock; viii (bg)Robert J. Hurt Landscape Photography; 129 Lester Lefkowitz/CORBIS; 130 (tl)Kindra Clineff/Index Stock Imagery, (tr)Stock Montage, (br)Kevin Flemming/CORBIS, (bl)Bettmann/CORBIS; 131 (tl)Bettmann/CORBIS, (tr)Library of Congress, Prints and Photographs Division, Washington, D.C., Reproduction No. LC-USZ62-109361/Library of Congress, (bl)SuperStock/age fotostock, (br)Joel Page/AP Images; 132 (bl)CORBIS, (br)Andrew Woodley/Alamy Images, (t)Adie Bush/Photonica/Getty Images; 133 (br)Jonathon Nourok/PhotoEdit, (tl)Lake County Museum/CORBIS, (tr)Ed Bishop/Index Stock Imagery; 134 (bcl)Charles Feil, (bcr)Dallas and John Heaton/CORBIS, (br)Siede Preis/Getty Images; 136-137 (bg)Charles Feil; 137 (b)Jerry Cooke/Animals Animals, (cl)Don Farrall/Photodisc/Getty Images, (cr)Siede Preis/Getty Images, (t)Phil Schermeister/CORBIS; 138 Dallas and John Heaton/CORBIS; 139 Jeff Greenberg/Alamy Images; 140 (bl)Owaki - Kulla/CORBIS, (t)Siede Preis/Getty Images, (cr)Charles Feil; 142 (bcl)The Granger Collection, New York, (bcr)SuperStock, (br)Earth Imaging/Stone/Getty Images; 142-143 (LesOp)E.R. Degginger/Dembinsky Photo Associates; 145 The Granger Collection, New York; 146 (r)Stewart Cohen/Blend Images/Alamy Images, (c)Blend Images/PunchStock, (l)Blend Images/Superstock; 147 (l)Pierre Tremblay/Masterfile, (r)SuperStock, (c)Masterfile Royalty-Free; 148-149 (bg)Earth Imaging/Stone/Getty Images; 149 (cr)E.R. Degginger/Dembinsky Photo Associates; 150 (bl)Grace Davies, (bcl)Courtesy of The Bancroft Library, University of California, Berkeley. [call number, BANC PIC 1980.098.73--PIC], (bcr)Alex Wong/Getty Images, (br)Paul O. Boisvert/Peter Arnold, Inc.; 150-151 (LesOp)Joseph Sohm; ChromoSohm Inc./CORBIS; 151 Grace Davies; 152 (tl)Bettmann/CORBIS, (tr)Courtesy of The Bancroft Library, University of California, Berkeley. [call number, BANC PIC 1980.098.73--PIC], (cr)The Granger Collection, New York, (cl)Photodisc/Getty Images, (bl)Atwater Kent Museum of Philadelphia/Courtesy of Historical Society of Pennsylvania Collection/Bridgeman Art Library; 153 (b)John McGrail/johnmcgrail.com, (tl)Blend Images/Alamy Images, (tr)Myrleen Ferguson Cate/PhotoEdit, (cl)Scott Rosen/Bill Smith Studio for MMH; 154 (tr)AP Images, (bl)Alex Wong/Getty Images, (br)Felicia Martinez/PhotoEdit; 155 (r)Grace Davies, (bl)Joel Simon/Stone/Getty Images; 156 (l)Elena Rooraid/PhotoEdit; 156-157 (bg)Paul O. Boisvert/Peter Arnold, Inc.; 157 (t)Richard T. Nowitz/CORBIS, (cr)Grace Davies; 160 Comstock Images/Jupiterimages; 161 David Graham/AP Images; 162 (tr)Sequoyah Birthplace Museum, (tl)National Portrait Gallery, Smithsonian Institution/Art Resource, Inc., (bl)Kim Kulish/CORBIS, (br)REUTERS/David Rae Morris; 163 (tl)William Lovelace/Express/Getty Images, (tr)Flip Schulke/CORBIS, (br)Bob Krist/CORBIS, (bl)AFP PHOTO/Paul J. Richards/NewsCom; 164 (b)GoodShoot/PunchStock, (tr)Creatas/SuperStock, (c)Robert Campbell/SuperStock; 165 (br)Millard H. Sharp/Photo Researchers, Inc., (bl)Gary Brettnacher/SuperStock, (tl)David Copeman/Alamy Images; 166 (bcl)Richard Stockton/Index Stock Imagery, (bcr)Stocktrek Images/Alamy Images, (br)DDB Stock Photography; 167 Lee Foster/Lonely Planet Images; 168-169 (bg)Jeff Greenberg/Alamy Images; 169 (l)Brownie Harris/CORBIS, (c)Richard Stockton/Index Stock Imagery; 169 PunchStock; 170-171 (bg)Michele Westmorland/Getty Images; 171 (t)Stocktrek Images/Alamy Images, (b)DDB Stock Photography; 172 Jeff Greenberg/Alamy Images; 174 (bcl)Melissa Farlow, (bcr)Harry Melchert/dpa/CORBIS, (br)Thinkstock/PunchStock, (bl)MMH; 174-175 (LesOp)Pictor/ImageState/Alamy Images; 176-177 Melissa Farlow; 178 (tr)Saxpix.com/age fotostock, (br)Bettmann/CORBIS, (tl)Jeff Greenberg/Unicorn Stock Photos; 180 (t)Thinkstock/PunchStock, (bg)Bruce Hands/Getty Images; 180-181 (b)Transparencies, Inc.; 181 (c)Melissa Farlow; 182 (bl)SuperStock, (bcl)Honey Salvadori/Alamy Images, (bcr)Bettmann/CORBIS, (br)Eliot Elisofon/Time Life Pictures/Getty Images; 182-183 (LesOp)Bettmann/CORBIS; 183 (br)SuperStock, (t)Burstein Collection/CORBIS; 184-185 (bg)Honey Salvadori/Alamy Images; 185 (t)Gayle Harper/In-Sight Photography, (b)Steven Mark Needham/Envision; 186 MPI/Hulton Archive/Getty Images, (tr)The Granger Collection, New York; 187 Marjorie Cotera/Daemmrich Associate/Bob Daemmrich Photography; 188 (bl)Randi Radcliff/AdMedia/NewsCom; 188-189 (bg)Eliot Elisofon/Time Life Pictures/Getty Images; 189 (tr)The Granger Collection, New York, (br)Bettmann/CORBIS; 190: Marjorie Cotera/Daemmrich Associate/Bob Daemmrich Photography; 192 (b)Michael Newman/PhotoEdit, (t)E Dygas/Getty Images; 193 Layne Kennedy; 194 (tr)The Granger Collection, New York, (bl)The Granger Collection, New York, (br)Midge Bolt/Midge Bolt Imaging; 195 (tr)The Granger Collection, New York, (tl)CORBIS/PunchStock, (bl)WorldSat International Inc./Science Source/Photo Researchers, Inc., (br)USFWS, National Wildlife Refuge System; 196 (tr)Eric Meola/Getty Images, (b)Brand X Pictures/PunchStock; 197 (b)Michael Conroy/AP Images, (tl)Rusty Hill/StockFood America, (tr)Andre Jenny/Alamy Images; 198 (bcr)Ilene MacDonald/Alamy Images, (br)Eric Meola/Getty Images; 201 The Granger Collection, New York; 202 (c)Wind Cave National Park/National Park Service, Wind Cave National Park; 202-203 (bg)Ilene MacDonald/Alamy Images; 203 (t)Wind Cave National Park/National Park Service, Wind Cave National Park; 204 Eric Meola/Getty Images; 206 (bcl)Tannen Maury/The Image Works, Inc., (bcr)Midwestock, (br)Kevin Fleming/CORBIS; 206-207 (LesOp)Lowell Georgia/CORBIS; 208-209 (bg)Andre Jenny/Alamy Images; 209 (r)Tannen Maury/The Image Works, Inc.; 210 Midwestock; 211 (bg)Grant Heilman Photography, (c)Sean Gallup/Getty Images; 212-213 (b)Kevin Fleming/CORBIS; 213 (c)Lowell Georgia/CORBIS; 214 (bl)Topham/The Image Works, Inc., (bcl)Bettmann/CORBIS, (bcr)Ilene MacDonald/Alamy Images, (br)Jeff Greenberg/Alamy Images; 214-215 (LesOp)The Ixtlan Artists Group; 215 Topham/The Image Works, Inc.; 216 Bettmann/CORBIS; 217 (tr)Bettmann/CORBIS, (bl)The Indianapolis Star, Rob Goebel/AP Images; 219 (cr)Courtesy of Irene McMullen, (bg)Ilene MacDonald/Alamy Images; 220 (tc)The Granger Collection, New York, (bl)Ionas Kaltenbach/Lonely Planet Images; 220-221 (bg)Amy Sancetta/AP Images; 221 (tr)Michael Kim/CORBIS, (cr)Bettmann/CORBIS; 222 Bettmann/CORBIS; 224 Ciaran Griffin/Getty Images; 225 Myrleen Ferguson Cate/PhotoEdit; 226 (tr)Royal Geographical Society, London, UK/Bridgeman Art Library, (bl)Jack Hollingsworth/Photodisc/Getty Images, (br)Scott Teven - PhotoHouston.com; 227 (tr)The Granger Collection, New York, (tl)Courtesy of the National Cowboys of Color Museum and Hall of Fame/Jon P. Uzzel, (bl)National Portrait Gallery, Smithsonian Institution/Art Resource, Inc., (bl)Bob Thomason/Getty Images; 228 (bl)Boone; D./CORBIS, (tr)Stefano Lunardi/Marka/age fotostock; 229 (br)Jack Kurtz/The Image Works, Inc., (bl)Photodisc/Getty Images, (t)Lake County (IL)Discovery Museum, Curt Teich Postcard Archives; 230 (bcl)Sitki Tarlan/Panoramic Images, (bcr)Michael Busselle/Digital Vision/SuperStock, (br)Tony Gervis/Robert Harding World Imagery/Getty Images; 232-233 (bg)Sitki Tarlan/Panoramic Images; 233 (t)Chris Howes/Wild Places Photography/Alamy Images; 234-235 (bg)Michael Busselle/Digital Vision/SuperStock; 235 (c)Brown Brothers; 236 (l)AP Images; 236-237 (bg)Tony Gervis/Robert Harding World Imagery/Getty Images; 237 (t)Sitki Tarlan/Panoramic Images; 240 (bc)David Frazier/PhotoEdit, (br)NASA/SSPL/The Image Works, Inc.; 240-241 (LesOp)Arthur Tilley/Getty Images; 241 (tr)Texas Energy Museum/Newsmakers/Getty Images; 242 (cl)Branson Reynolds, (cr)David Frazier/PhotoEdit, (br)Aaron Haupt/Photo Researchers, Inc.; 242-243 (bg)Bob Daemmrich/The Image Works, Inc.; 243 (br)Adam Woolfitt/Robert Harding Picture Library Ltd/Alamy Images, (cl)Jack Parsons Photography, (tl)eStock Photo/Alamy Images; 244 (b)George F Mobley/National Geographic Image Collection, (cl)Jagadeesh Nv/Reuters/CORBIS; 245 (b)NASA/SSPL/The Image Works, Inc., (t)Branson Reynolds; 246 (bl)SuperStock/age fotostock, (bcl)The Granger Collection, New York, (bcr)Mike Mcgovern/Index Stock Imagery, (br)Jim Olive / Stockyard Photos; 246-247 (LesOp)Owen Franken/CORBIS; 247 SuperStock/age fotostock; 248-249 (bg)The Granger Collection, New York; 249 (tl)Robert Glusic/Pixtal/age fotostock, (br)Archivo Jose Luis Dorado/Godo-Foto; 250 (b)Mike Mcgovern/Index Stock Imagery, (tr)Tony Vaccaro/Hulton Archive/Getty Images; 252 (t)Lisa Law/The Image Works, Inc., (cr)AM Corporation/Alamy Images; 253 (b)Jim Olive / Stockyard Photos, (t)Owen Franken/CORBIS; 254 Lisa Law/The Image Works; 256 TongRo Image Stock/Jupiterimages; 257 Steven Georges/Press-Telegram/CORBIS; 258 (tl)Gail Mooney/Masterfile, (tr)Wolfgang Kaehler Photography, (br)Lorenz Britt/Alamy Images; 259 (tl)The Huntington Library, Art Collections, and Botanical Gardens, San Marino, California/SuperStock, (tr)The Granger Collection, New York, (br)Jim Sugar/CORBIS, (bl)Roger Ressmeyer/CORBIS; 260 (tr)Joel W. Rogers/CORBIS, (bl)Gary Crabbe/Alamy Images, (br)Comstock Images/Alamy Images; 261 (br)Mark Junak/Getty Images, (tr)Staffan Widstrand/CORBIS, (bl)Lake County Museum/CORBIS; 262 (bcl)John Elk III Photography, (bcr)Adam Teitelbaum/AFP/Getty Images, (br)Bananastock/PictureQuest/Jupiterimages; 264 (bl)Brand X/PunchStock; 264-265 (bg)John Elk III Photography; 265 (cr)Anthony Mercieca/Photo Researchers, Inc.; 266 Adam Teitelbaum/AFP/Getty Images; 267 Gunter Marx Photography/CORBIS; 268 (t)Bananastock/PictureQuest/Jupiterimages, (cl)Wisconsin Historical Society/Everett Collection; 269 (c)John Elk III Photography, (b)John Shaw/Photo Researchers, Inc.; 272 (bl)David R. Frazier Photolibrary, Inc./Alamy Images, (bcr)Walt Disney/Kobal Collection, (br)David Young-Wolff/Getty Images; 272-273 (LesOp)Nevada Wier/CORBIS; 273 (br)Gibson Stock Photography, (bc)David R. Frazier Photolibrary, Inc./Alamy Images; 276 Walt Disney/Kobal Collection; 277 (br)Natalie Fobes/CORBIS, (t)Transtock Inc./Alamy Images; 278 (bl)Michael S. Yamashita/CORBIS, (br)Stewart Cohen/Pam Ostrow/Blend Images/Getty Images; 279 (bl)David Young-Wolff/Getty Images, (cr)Nevada Wier/CORBIS; 280 (bl)Vince Streano/CORBIS, (br)Garrett Cheen/The Livingston Enterprise/AP Images, (bc)Torre Abbey, Torquay, Devon, UK/Bridgeman Art Library; 280-281 (LesOp)Vince Streano/CORBIS; 281 (b)Kevin Red Star Gallery; 282 (tr)Collection of the Oakland Museum of California, Gift of Paul S. Taylor; 282-283 (bg)Trevor Wood/Getty Images; 283 (tr)Torre Abbey, Torquay, Devon, UK/Bridgeman Art Library; 284 (t)Danita Delimont/Alamy Images, (b)Paul A. Souders/CORBIS; 285 (bl)Garrett Cheen/The Livingston Enterprise/AP Images, (r)Vince Streano/CORBIS; 286 (c)Garrett Cheen/The Livingston Enterprise/AP Images; 288 Fancy/Veer; BKCOV Imagemore/SuperStock.

ACKNOWLEDGMENTS

Grateful acknowledgment is given to the following authors and publishers. Every effort has been made to trace the ownership of all copyrighted material and to secure the necessary permissions to reprint these selections. In the case of some selections for which acknowledgment is not given, extensive research has failed to locate the copyright holders.